Air Fryer

Cookbook for Beginners UK

Quick and Mouthwatering Air Fryer Recipes with Vivid Full-colour Images | Tips and Tricks for Time and Energy Savings | UK Meas.

Ellie Peacock

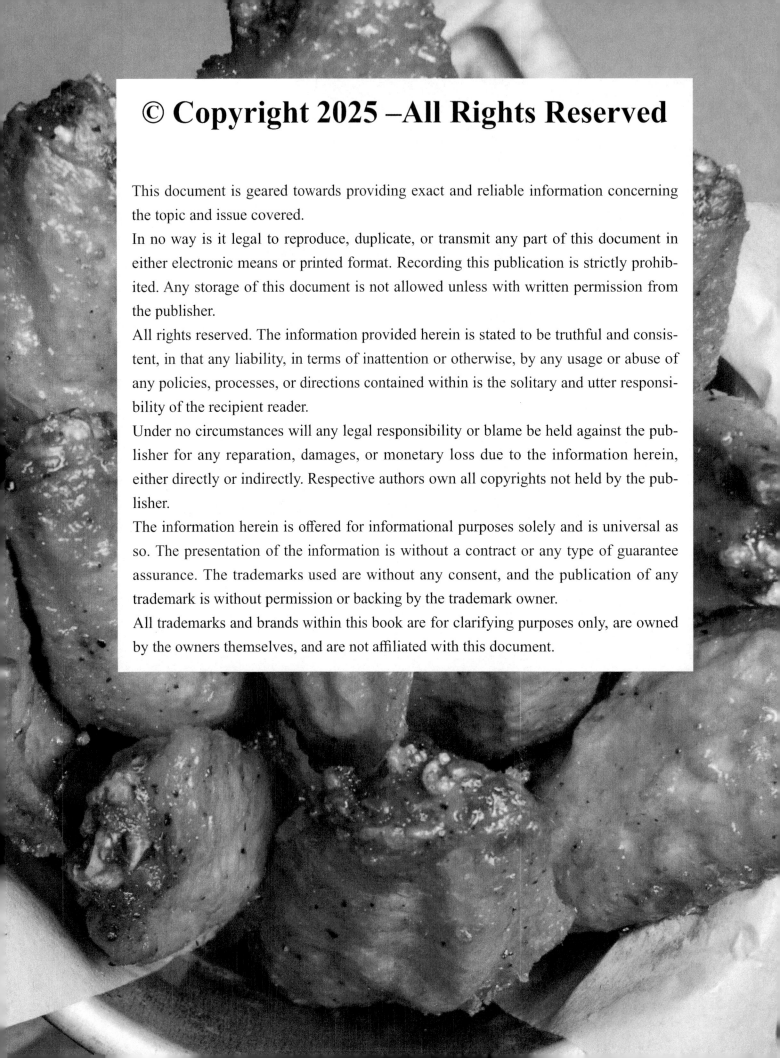

Table of Contents

Introduction

Welcome to a world where hot air transforms simple ingredients into crispy delights! The realm of air frying is not as new as one might imagine. Journey back a few decades, and you'll find the origins of air frying rooted in Western Europe. The promise? Delivering the beloved crispness of fried foods with less to no oil, creating a revolutionary way to savor our favorites while sidelining some of the guilt.

An air fryer is a revolutionary kitchen appliance designed to produce crispy dishes without immersing them in oil. Yes, you heard it right - the oil. Since its debut in 2010, this appliance has graced countless kitchens globally, with its popularity only poised to expand.

Fast forward to today, and this kitchen gadget has danced its way into hearts and homes across the globe. From the bustling streets of New York to the tranquil towns of New Zealand, the air fryer is not just a passing trend—it's become a countertop mainstay. Its growing popularity isn't merely due to its promise of healthier meals; the efficiency, versatility, and sheer joy of experimentation have made it an indispensable tool in the modern kitchen.

While many may perceive the air fryer as a mere frying tool, its culinary catalog extends far beyond. From frying to roasting, grilling to baking, this versatile device easily crafts delectable dishes. The secret? Its "Rapid Air Technology" circulates hot air with precision, replicating the effect of submerging food in a hot oil bath.

The standout feature? It can use almost 80% less of the cooking oil. Plus, the speed is unmatched – meals are ready in a fraction of the conventional time. A cooking game-changer, indeed.

Fundamentals of Air Fryer

We must understand this unique world of air frying using hot air currents! Picture this: a kitchen where the traditional frying undergoes a futuristic twist, coming up with crunchy delicacies without the greasy results. The air fryer isn't just a tool; it's an experience, a journey of flavors waiting to be unveiled. This chapter explores its design to the ballet of hot air inside, a gadget that has redefined the art of frying foods.

What is an Air Fryer?

Imagine enjoying your favorite crispy treats cooked with hot air instead of plenty of oil. Then comes the air fryer, the kitchen magician who has been redefining the art of frying for countless food enthusiasts. The appliance uses the principles of convection, where a mechanical fan directs hot air to circulate and cook the ingredients within the chamber. It still cooks amazing foods using the Maillard effect, named after the French chemist Louis-Camille Maillard, who unveiled its secrets in 1912. This reaction between reducing sugars and amino acids gives foods like seared steaks, cookies, and pan-fried meat their signature flavors and tantalizing aromas.

Remarkably, the air fryer achieves these results using less to no oil, circulating hot air at temperatures as high as 392° F.

It graciously trims down oil content by an impressive 80%, making the results a healthy option. Outfitted with user-friendly features, from timer adjustments to precise temperature controls, each brand usually comes with a basket on a drip tray, ensuring minimal mess.

The appliance serves you well, especially when using it at home. When it comes to many people, the same technique will apply, but you set your ingredients in specialized air crisper trays and use a convection oven to cook. They both use similar cooking techniques, and the air fryer has a principle of crispy perfection with minimal oil.

What Are Some of the Unique Features of the Device?

Travel-Friendly Design (portable): Your new air fryer isn't just an appliance; it's a portable kitchen companion. Whether moving from cabinet to countertop or even a trip to a friend's house for a cooking expedition, its design ensures seamless transitions.

Precision Temperature Regulation: Say goodbye to guesswork! With automatic temperature control, your meals reach consistent perfection. Adjust to your desired temperature, and the fryer ensures your dish always hits that sweet spot.

User-Friendly Digital Interface: Cooking skills or not, your air fryer doesn't discriminate. Thanks to its intuitive digital touch screen, you are in for a special experience. Regardless of the model, a few taps on the panel stand between you and an amazing dish.

Alert System: Overcooked meals? A thing of the past! With the integrated timer and buzzer, you'll always be in the know. These timely audio signals mean you can relax while your fryer does its thing, alerting you when meal perfection is achieved.

Effortless Cooking with Presets: The appliance comes with some cooking presets, easing your work in the kitchen. Your air fryer comes pre-loaded with settings for popular dishes. Select, start, and sit back - your fryer knows the drill!

Is Frying without Oil Achievable?

Can you truly achieve that crispy goodness without drenching food in excessive oil? This question is challenging to answer because oil is more than just a cooking medium. It's a flavor enhancer, a texture transformer, and the secret sauce to many recipes. Yes, certain meals, particularly meats like poultry, occasionally require a touch of oil to get the best flair. However, the air fryer has amazing considerations with a minimalistic approach to oil. Many recipes you prepare will need mere spritzes from a cooking spray or a thin mist from an oil mister. Gone are the days of foods deep-fried in cups of oil!

Interestingly, the art of frying without excessive oil is anchored in the Maillard reaction (explained in the previous paragraphs above). It is a chemical reaction where proteins and sugars, under heat's influence, get transformed to acquire rich flavors, tantalizing aromas, and a pleasant crispness. To achieve the Maillard magic:

- **Heat:** Central to the Maillard ballet, performance is realized at temperatures of 300°F (≈148°C) and higher, leading to that golden-brown appeal. Oil is not a prerequisite, but ensure your ingredients do not contain excessive moisture.
- **Moisture:** There is a zone of hydration that suits well for this Maillard reaction. Too damp may prevent browning; overly dry, and you end up with a charred outcome. Since air fryers use hot air circulation, moisture content should be balanced.
- **Time:** Carefully play around with the timing; extending the cooking duration at lower temperatures can yield similar Maillard marvels. With prolonged cooking time, there is a gradual release of excess moisture while progressively building the necessary heat.

Benefits of Using It

Come closer if you're still wondering about the perks of welcoming this gadget appliance to your kitchen. Let's explore the whole art of air frying and unearth the myriad treasures it holds:

A Healthier Horizon with the Use of Less Oil

Wave goodbye to calories that come with the use of excessive oil. With the air fryer, you're venturing into a realm of eating without much heavy weight of guilt. Lavish pools of oil become relics of the past. Achieve that golden crunch with a mere mist of oil, cutting down fats by up to 80%. Using the air fryer system eliminates unhealthy oils, and you can comfortably enjoy your fries/chips. Your waistline and heart send their thanks!

Time Is Truly on Your Side

Modern life is full of busy schedules and may call for efficiency, and the air fryer answers. Witness the marvel of dishes being ready in nearly half the time of traditional methods. Every minute saved is another savory bite or a moment with loved ones. An air fryer does not require the user to always remain alert during cooking. All you need to do is to set the temperature and cooking time and only return occasionally to shake the fryer basket for uniform cooking.

A Versatile Appliance

The gadget is amazing at achieving a symphony of dishes! From crispy fries to succulent chicken, delightful pastries to roasted veggies, its range is vast and varied. Whether you're preparing breakfast, lunch, dinner, or a midnight snack, the air fryer plays the perfect tune. You can gracefully transition into baking, grilling, or broiling roles.

Safe and Sound

You are now safe in your kitchen. No more of the unnecessary splattering of oil and potential burns. Enclosed and automated, the air fryer ensures your experience is safe, reducing the risks associated with traditional frying.

Easy Cleanup

The grand finale? Who doesn't like having less to deal with once you have enjoyed a delicious meal? The air fryer ensures that you have a kitchen devoid of greasy aftermath. The drip collection basket in the air fryer collects whatever small amount of oil n is released while cooking. All residue oil is collected in the drip basket, and cleaning this basket ensures complete cleaning of the cooking place after the cooking is done. Most components are dishwasher-friendly, turning the tedious task of cleaning into a swift task. Most people find it easy to clean the components under a running tap.

Push, Play, and Relish

The air fryer is user-friendly. Gone are the days of hovering over sizzling pans. With intuitive controls, the air fryer is your kitchen friend. Set time and temperature depending on the recipe, press the start button, and let the culinary magic unfurl. This is also a farewell to oil splatters and unexpected burns!

Convenient to Use

You use electricity to run the air fryers, and you can easily place the fryer in any convenient place in the house, plug it into the nearest electricity source, and start enjoying hassle-free cooking. Being a very compact device, it is easy to maneuver to the desired place and equally easy to operate.

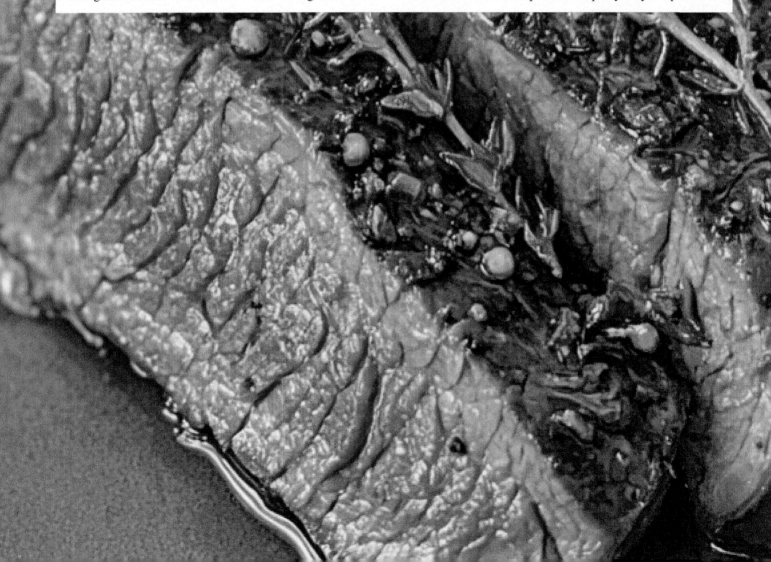

Consistent Flavorful Fiesta

Don't be fooled by its scant oil use. Always expect a harmonious blend of flavors and textures each time you get in the kitchen. With precise temperature controls and even air circulation, the dishes you prepare are consistently delectable, making every meal a standing ovation. You will always achieve the fried taste and texture.

Odor-Free Cooking

One distinct advantage is the absence of that lingering fried aroma. Your kitchen stays fresh-smelling even after cooking.

Withstanding Heavy Cooking

Whether you're cooking for a daily meal or a feast, its robust design seamlessly handles light and heavy-duty cooking.

Durability

Crafted with durable metal and premium-grade plastic, it's about performance and longevity.

Pocket-friendly cooking and energy efficiency

Air fryers are considerably less expensive. Several models are available, and you can easily select one that meets your needs. Air fryers also run on electricity, meaning they are environmentally friendly and save you on electric bills since they are efficient in using energy.

Tips to Prepare Healthy Foods in Air Fryer

1. You can easily cook vegetables in an Air Fryer. To enjoy the best experience, soak veggies, especially harder ones. Set to soak in cold water for 20 minutes. Use a kitchen towel to dry them afterward.

2. Try out air roasting to prepare some of your winter favorites

3. At halfway of your cooking duration, it is advisable to flip or shake your foods. This ensures uniform or even browning or crisping.

   Also, do a Mid-Cook Oil Spritz. Spraying a light oil mist on most foods halfway through cooking enhances the result. This is particularly true for coated foods or to cover any lingering flour patches.

4. Read the manual before you decide to bake recipes that call for that.

5. All recipes are designed for the different air fryer models. So ensure you cook until you attain the desired doneness. If more time is needed, adjust the time accordingly since some ingredients may vary in firmness and size.

6. Be careful with the cooking time since it may vary with the specific model of the air fryer, size of ingredients or people to serve, pre-preparation of food, and many other factors.

Shorter cooking cycles may require you to preheat your air fryer for 4 minutes since you will need to increase the cooking time by 4 minutes if you set your ingredients in a cold air fryer basket.

7. Brush your food and cooking basket using good quality oil spray to ensure that you don't experience difficulties during the cleaning process.

8. Avoid Aerosol Sprays. Brands like Pam, while convenient, can harm your air fryer's container due to mismatched chemical interactions, leading to chipping.

9. Avoid Crowding your air fryer. For that perfect crispy finish, refrain from overloading your air fryer. Overcrowding prevents even air circulation. Either cook in batches or consider a larger device for bigger meals.

10. The Pause and Resume. On opening the basket mid-cook, the air fryer may pause, but it'll resume once the basket is replaced.

11. When frying very fatty foods, white smoke might emerge. Add a couple of tablespoons of water to the container base to counter this. Alternatively, a bread slice at the base can absorb excess grease, especially when cooking items like bacon.

12. Beware of Lightweight Foods. Given the robust fan in many air fryers, lightweight items can get tossed around. Ensure these items are secured or consider ways to prevent them from flying and clogging the fan.

13. When it comes to meats, accuracy is crucial. Invest in a good quality thermometer to ensure perfectly cooked proteins every time.

Step-By-Step of Air Frying

Ah, so you've decided to work with the air fryer, a modern innovation promising to revolutionize your kitchen experience! Just like mastering any new dance, getting in step with your air fryer requires a rhythm, a touch of grace, and passion. Let's see the steps:

The Warm-Up

Unbox and Admire: Gently remove the unit and accessories from the box, admiring its sleek design and curves. Familiarize yourself with its buttons, basket, and any accompanying accessories.

Clean all washable parts and pieces of the air fryer that will handle your food. Accomplishing this before storage speeds up your recipe preparation when ready to start.

Find Your Space

Positioning: Ensure you position your air fryer on a flat surface or countertop, preferably away from any wall or appliance. Give it room to breathe without stuffing it along with other things!

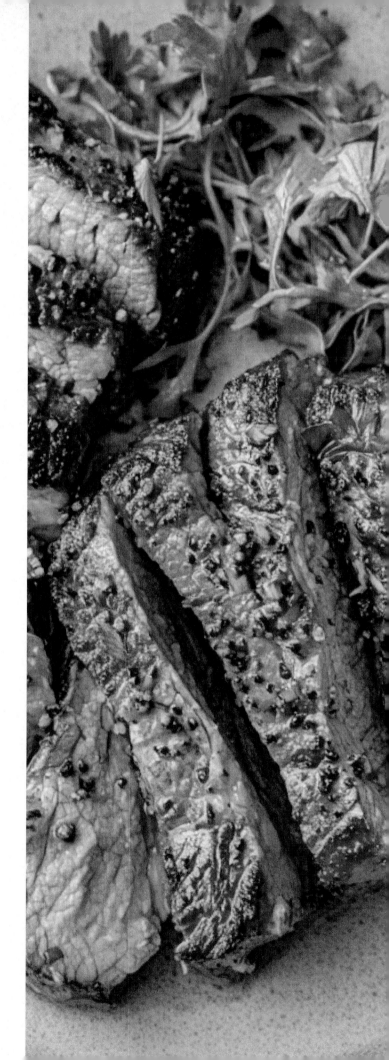

Preparing to Cook

- **Moisture Watch:** For that impeccable crisp, ensure any excess moisture, especially from marinated meats or naturally watery foods like potatoes, is thoroughly patted away.
- **The Oil Equation:** While the air fryer champions minimal oil use, certain foods might benefit from a touch. If you opt out of oil, a spritz of non-stick cooking spray on the food or basket can be your shield against stickiness.
- **Uniformity Matters:** Aim for consistent sizes in your cut ingredients when prepping your ingredients. This isn't just culinary aesthetics; it's about ensuring every part cooks uniformly.
- **Clean Slate:** Before the cooking process begins, ensure no leftover residue or fat drippings from prior uses. This prevents unnecessary spattering and potential smoky messes.
- You may decide to use aluminum foil for easy cleaning.
- **Give Them Space:** Avoid overcrowding the ingredients, allowing them ample space for hot air to circulate, even if it means multiple showtimes (or batches). Such will achieve proper and even cooking.
- **Preheating:** If your model has a preheat function, it's fantastic! If not, preheat. Just as a musician tunes their instrument, preheat the air fryer to the desired temperature for about 3-5 minutes, setting the stage for the culinary experience ahead.

During the Cooking Process

- **Recipe Flexibility:** Remember, provided recipes and their cooking times are more guidelines than strict rules. Your ingredients might vary in size, or perhaps you've tailored quantities to your liking. Additionally, 'perfectly done' is subjective and varies from one person to another. Therefore, be prepared to adjust cooking times slightly based on these variables. The density of food inside the fryer can also affect its cooking duration.

- **Set the desired temperature for different recipes**
- **Intermission Act:** As you reach the midpoint of your cooking process, it's time for a little rotation. For bite-sized ingredients like fries, a gentle basket shake will do. For the main or larger portions, like a juicy steak or a fillet of fish, turn them over to ensure an even performance.

After Cooking

- Checking Doneness: As the timer nears its end, check out the inside. Depending on your dish, you might be looking for a golden-brown finish or a certain softness.
- Remove the basket from the drawer before you get hold of your food.
- Use the collected juices for preparing delicious sauces and marinades
- Unplug the unit from the wall unit, allow it to cool, and clean the basket and drawer for next use.

Always Remember

The air fryer isn't just a kitchen gadget; it's a portal to culinary adventures. While it's known for recreating traditional fried delights, its capabilities don't stop there. This guide will take you beyond the conventional, showcasing the diverse dishes waiting to be discovered. View this great device as a canvas for healthy, creative cookery. From frying to roasting, steaming to baking, let your imagination and this air fryer transform your kitchen escapades into delicacies of flavors and textures.

The Different Functions

Your air fryer arrives neatly packed, complete with an instruction manual ensuring easy assembly. Some brands come with a recipe booklet.

When the itch to cook strikes and you have your ingredients lined up, just pop them into the basket and slide them into the fryer. Some recipes might prompt you to give your fryer a quick preheat. With the basket snugly in place, dial in your desired temperature and set your timer. Then, let the culinary magic commence.

Here's a glimpse into the multifaceted cooking styles your air fryer can effortlessly execute:

Fry

Step 1: Preheat Prelude - Begin by warming up your air fryer to the desired temperature. Most dishes thrive at a temperature range of 350°F to 400°F.

Step 2: Oil Spray - Lightly coat your chosen ingredients with a touch of oil or cooking spray. This ensures a crispy, golden exterior.

Step 3: Ingredients in the Basket - Place the ingredients in the basket, ensuring they have space to rotate. Crowding might lead to an uneven fry.

Step 4: Mid-way shake - Halfway through, gently shake the basket to rotate ingredients, ensuring a consistent golden hue.

Step 5: End - Once your ingredients have rotated to crispy perfection, carefully remove them. Serve immediately for the best crunch!

Roast

Step 1: Preheating - Preheat the air fryer to the roasting temperature, typically between 325°F to 375°F.

Step 2: Seasoned Performance - Season your chosen ingredients. For vegetables, a drizzle of oil, salt, and pepper might serve well. Meats might require a more extensive marinade or rub.

Step 3: Set Ingredients - Place your ingredients in the basket, ensuring even spacing for a uniform roast.

Step 4: Rotate & Revel - Midway, turn the ingredients to ensure all sides get their moment under the hot air.

Step 5: Final stage - Once roasted to your desired level, remove and let the dish cool briefly before serving.

Bake

Step 1: Initial Preheating - Preheat the air fryer to your baking temperature. This could vary based on the dish but is often between 300°F to 350°F.

Step 2: Preparation Solo - Prepare your batter or dough as per your recipe.

Step 3: Mold & Set - If you're using a mold or pan (like for muffins or cakes), ensure it's air fryer compatible. Fill it up and place it inside.

Step 4: Bake & Wait - Let the ingredients bake. Resist the urge to peek too often.

Step 5: Final stage - Once baked to perfection, remove, let it cool slightly, and then enjoy your airy and fluffy bake!

Grill

Step 1: Tuning and Preheating - Preheat the air fryer to a high temperature, usually around 400°F, similar to grilling conditions.

Step 2: Marination - Prepare your meats or vegetables by marinating or seasoning them.

Step 3: Basket Brilliance - Place the ingredients in the basket. For an authentic grill feel, you can use an air fryer grill pan if you have one.

Step 4: Mid-grill Maneuver - Halfway through, flip your ingredients for even grill marks and cooking.

Step 5: Final Stages - Once grilled to your satisfaction, remove the dish, allow it to cool for a few minutes, and then enjoy!

Tips for Using Accessories

While the fryer can certainly work well on its own, adding accessories gives you amazing results! Here are some of the accessories.

1. **Air Fryer Basket:** Ensure it's clean and dry before each use. When cooking, give ingredients ample space for that golden crisp finish.

2. **Air Fryer Baking Pan:** Ideal for muffins, cakes, and bread. Lightly grease before pouring in the batter to ensure nothing sticks.

3. **Air Fryer Double Layer Rack:** When one layer isn't enough! Ensure even spacing on both levels for uniform cooking.

4. **Air Fryer Grill Pan:** Perfect for that grilled finish on meats and veggies. Clean those grooves post-use for an optimum grilling experience.

5. **Air Fryer Food Separator:** Cooking fries and chicken together? Keep flavors distinct with this tool. One on the left and the other on the right.

6. **Cooking Oil Filter:** Use this to ensure your oil is free from particles, especially if reusing.

7. **Charcoal Barbecue Filter:** Replace regularly to keep any smoky or lingering odors at bay.

8. **Lift Lid:** A safer way to check on your food without pausing the cooking process.

9. **Bamboo Cutting Board:** A sustainable choice for prepping when you need to cut your ingredients. Remember to clean and dry after each use.

10. **Frying Pan Cover:** Keeps your countertop clean by catching any unexpected splashes or pops.

11. **Cookie Sheet Liners:** Perfect for keeping delicate baked goods warm. Remember, metal cookie cutters can scratch them, so be gentle!

12. **Sear Plate:** For those times you crave that perfect sear on your steak or fish.

13. **Removable Crumb Tray:** Regularly empty and clean this tray to keep your fryer functioning flawlessly.

14. **Silicone Muffin Molds:** Use these for perfectly shaped muffins and cupcakes. A light grease before pouring batter ensures easy release.

Straight from the Store

The moment has arrived. Opening the packaging, revealing what promises to be your new kitchen friend: The Air Fryer. What is in the box

The Air Fryer Unit:

Sturdy and sleek, this main unit houses the heart of your air fryer. It has an intuitive design, often fitted with digital screens and dials.

Included Accessories:

Removable Air Fryer Basket: The essential vessel, perfect for everything from crispy fries to delicate seafood.

Cooking Chamber: This is where you place your food to cook. Depending on the brand and model, it could be a single tray or multi-tray.

We also have the convection fan, exhaust system, and heating elements.

User Manual: This isn't just a booklet; it's your guide to understanding your appliance's habits, charms, and full potential.

Warranty Card: Keep this safe.

Acquiring Ingredients: Curating Your Culinary Palette

1. **Go to the Local Farmers' Markets:** A treasure trove of fresh produce. Here, veggies and fruits are fresh.
2. **Butchers & Fisheries:** For the freshest cuts of meat and catches of the day. Remember, freshness translates to flavor.

3. **Ethnic Groceries:** Spice up your air fryer adventures. From Asian sesame oils to Middle Eastern spices, these stores hold the key to global cuisines.
4. **Bulk Stores:** For your grains, seeds, and dried fruits. It is not only economical but also eco-friendly if you bring your own containers.
5. **Specialty Stores:** Sometimes, a dish demands a specific ingredient, be it truffle oil or a rare cheese. Specialty stores are your go-to for these unique items.
6. **Your Own Garden:** Nothing beats the joy of plucking a tomato off your plant or snipping fresh herbs straight into your air fryer basket.

Cleaning and Caring for Your Air Fryer

If you don't clean and maintain the air fryer well, it won't last for long.

How to Clean Your Air Fryer?

1. Unplug the air fryer from the source of power or wall socket. Allow the appliance to cool completely.
2. Utilize a damp cloth to wipe the appliance's exterior.
3. Remove all removable parts like the air fryer pan, tray, and basket, and wash them using hot water and a dishwasher soap.
4. Take a sponge or damp cloth and clean the inner section.
5. Use a brush to scrub any ingredients that tick in the air fryer.
6. Allow all accessories to air dry before returning them to the unit.
7. Once clean, ensure you store it well.

Maintaining Your Air Fryer:

1. Check the power chord to ensure it is not damaged to avoid accidents.

2. Ensure no debris in the fryer before you start cooking.
3. Set your air fryer on a flat countertop.
4. Set it away from the wall or another gadget. Maintain a 4-inch distance to the nearest element.
5. Check all components to ensure they are in good condition.
6. If any is damaged, let it be repaired or replaced.

Frequently Asked Questions & Notes

1. **I see white or black smoke coming out of my air fryer. Should I be alarmed?** White smoke typically arises from an accumulation of fat or excess oil pooling at the fryer's bottom. A quick cleaning should resolve this. Black smoke, however, signals a problem with the machine itself. In this case, immediately unplug and seek professional repair.
2. **My food is not crisping. Is it an oil issue?** Yes, if your food turns out dry, chewy, or lacks that golden crisp, it's likely due to insufficient oil. Remember, air frying creates a crunchy texture due to the tiny circulating oil molecules. When these are absent, you're just baking, leading to a blander outcome. Always follow the recipe's oil instructions.
3. **There's a lingering smell in my air fryer. What to do?** Proper cleaning post-use is your best defense against lingering odors. Soak and scrub the fryer basket and any accessories in hot, soapy water. Ensure thorough rinsing and drying before your next cooking.
4. **Can I line my air fryer with baking paper or aluminum foil?** While you can, be cautious. The air fryer's powerful fans might cause these linings to flutter onto the heating element, risking burns. If you must use them, perforate them for better airflow.
5. **Do I need to preheat?** Though not always necessary, preheating helps in achieving a consistent cooking result. If unsure, simply warm up your fryer to the desired temperature for a few minutes before introducing your ingredients.
6. **Is there a risk of overloading my air fryer?** Yes! Overcrowding hampers even cooking. If you're cooking for a large group, either cook in batches or consider investing in a larger air fryer.

4-Week Meal Plan

Week 1

Day 1:
Breakfast: Traditional English Breakfast
Lunch: Creamy Cauliflower Potato Soup
Snack: Parmesan Courgette Chips
Dinner: Air Fryer Curry Chicken Drumsticks
Dessert: Raspberry Chocolate Lava Cake

Day 2:
Breakfast: Walnut Banana Muffins
Lunch: Vegan Shepherd's Pie
Snack: Sweet Potato Chips
Dinner: Mustard Pork Chops with Potatoes
Dessert: Hazelnut Cookies

Day 3:
Breakfast: Mini Cheese Chorizo Frittatas
Lunch: Cheesy Stuffed Peppers
Snack: Simple French Fries
Dinner: Pork Belly with Golden Syrup Sauce
Dessert: Traditional Cranachan

Day 4:
Breakfast: Bacon Butty Sandwich
Lunch: Rosemary Potato Soup
Snack: Lemon Cream Scones
Dinner: Sweet & Sour Flank Steak
Dessert: Fluffy Orange Soufflé

Day 5:
Breakfast: Pumpkin Scones
Lunch: Green Asparagus Soup
Snack: Puff Pastry Pigs in a Blanket
Dinner: Honey Glazed Salmon
Dessert: Banana Cake

Day 6:
Breakfast: Scrambled Eggs with Tomatoes
Lunch: Cheese Vegetable Pie
Snack: Crispy Potatoes and Asparagus
Dinner: Tasty Rib-Eye Steak
Dessert: Mini Cherry Tart

Day 7:
Breakfast: Cloud Eggs on Toast
Lunch: Cream and Cheese Stuffed Pumpkin
Snack: Grilled Courgette Cheese Rolls
Dinner: Rack of Lamb with Mint Pesto
Dessert: Banana Bread with Vanilla Ricotta & Raspberries Compote

Week 2

Day 1:
Breakfast: Orange Blueberry Muffins
Lunch: Cheesy Vegetable Casserole
Snack: Cinnamon Apple Crisps
Dinner: Spiced Whole Duck
Dessert: Maple Pears with Roasted Pecan Nuts

Day 2:
Breakfast: Eggy Bread
Lunch: Chili Parsnip and Cauliflower Soup
Snack: Cheesy Beans On Toast
Dinner: Crispy Breaded Chicken Breasts
Dessert: Easy Gingerbread Bundt Cake

Day 3:
Breakfast: Breakfast Yoghurt Carrot Muffins
Lunch: Thyme Roasted Vegetables
Snack: Mini Crumpets Pizza
Dinner: Air Fryer Herbed Salmon
Dessert: Apple Oatmeal Cookies

Day 4:
Breakfast: Creamy Fried Squid and Egg Yolks
Lunch: Roasted Broccoli and Stilton Soup
Snack: Chocolate Pear Flapjacks
Dinner: Air Fryer Mustard Pork Tenderloin
Dessert: Raspberry Cupcakes

Day 5:
Breakfast: Pumpkin Scones
Lunch: Cream Carrot Soup with Pancetta Bread
Snack: Sweet Potato Chips
Dinner: Simple Herb Roast Beef
Dessert: Toffee Apple Bread with Cream Pudding

Day 6:
Breakfast: Scottish Oats Porridge with Blueberries
Lunch: Cheese Vegetable Pie
Snack: Parmesan Carrot Fries
Dinner: Honey Mustard Glazed Chicken Wings
Dessert: Traditional Cranachan

Day 7:
Breakfast: Walnut Banana Muffins
Lunch: Green Asparagus Soup
Snack: Cheesy Hash Brown Casserole
Dinner: Rack of Lamb with Mint Pesto
Dessert: Raspberry Chocolate Lava Cake

Week 3

Day 1:
Breakfast: Mini Cheese Chorizo Frittatas
Lunch: Creamy Cauliflower Potato Soup
Snack: Lemon Cream Scones
Dinner: Sweet & Sour Flank Steak
Dessert: Fluffy Orange Soufflé

Day 2:
Breakfast: Walnut Banana Muffins
Lunch: Thyme Roasted Vegetables
Snack: Parmesan Courgette Chips
Dinner: Pork Belly with Golden Syrup Sauce
Dessert: Hazelnut Cookies

Day 3:
Breakfast: Pumpkin Scones
Lunch: Green Asparagus Soup
Snack: Sweet Potato Chips
Dinner: Tasty Rib-Eye Steak
Dessert: Traditional Cranachan

Day 4:
Breakfast: Cloud Eggs on Toast
Lunch: Cheese Vegetable Pie
Snack: Simple French Fries
Dinner: Air Fryer Curry Chicken Drumsticks
Dessert: Raspberry Cupcakes

Day 5:
Breakfast: Orange Blueberry Muffins
Lunch: Roasted Broccoli and Stilton Soup
Snack: Grilled Courgette Cheese Rolls
Dinner: Honey Glazed Salmon
Dessert: Maple Pears with Roasted Pecan Nuts

Day 6:
Breakfast: Scrambled Eggs with Tomatoes
Lunch: Vegan Shepherd's Pie
Snack: Cheesy Beans On Toast
Dinner: Rack of Lamb with Mint Pesto
Dessert: Raspberry Chocolate Lava Cake

Day 7:
Breakfast: Eggy Bread
Lunch: Chili Parsnip and Cauliflower Soup
Snack: Puff Pastry Pigs in a Blanket
Dinner: Mustard Pork Chops with Potatoes
Dessert: Toffee Apple Bread with Cream Pudding

Week 4

Day 1:
Breakfast: Breakfast Yoghurt Carrot Muffins
Lunch: Rosemary Potato Soup
Snack: Parmesan Carrot Fries
Dinner: Crispy Breaded Chicken Breasts
Dessert: Raspberry Chocolate Lava Cake

Day 2:
Breakfast: Mini Cheese Chorizo Frittatas
Lunch: Green Asparagus Soup
Snack: Sweet Potato Chips
Dinner: Pork Belly with Golden Syrup Sauce
Dessert: Banana Cake

Day 3:
Breakfast: Pumpkin Scones
Lunch: Cheese Vegetable Pie
Snack: Lemon Cream Scones
Dinner: Air Fryer Curry Chicken Drumsticks
Dessert: Easy Gingerbread Bundt Cake

Day 4:
Breakfast: Cloud Eggs on Toast
Lunch: Cream and Cheese Stuffed Pumpkin
Snack: Grilled Courgette Cheese Rolls
Dinner: Tasty Rib-Eye Steak
Dessert: Fluffy Orange Soufflé

Day 5:
Breakfast: Orange Blueberry Muffins
Lunch: Chili Parsnip and Cauliflower Soup
Snack: Puff Pastry Pigs in a Blanket
Dinner: Honey Glazed Salmon
Dessert: Raspberry Cupcakes

Day 6:
Breakfast: Eggy Bread
Lunch: Roasted Broccoli and Stilton Soup
Snack: Parmesan Courgette Chips
Dinner: Rack of Lamb with Mint Pesto
Dessert: Traditional Cranachan

Day 7:
Breakfast: Walnut Banana Muffins
Lunch: Creamy Cauliflower Potato Soup
Snack: Cheesy Beans On Toast
Dinner: Simple Herb Roast Beef
Dessert: Toffee Apple Bread with Cream Pudding

Chapter 1 Breakfast Recipes

Traditional English Breakfast

⏱ **Prep Time: 5 minutes**   🍲 **Cook: 10 minutes**   ❧ **Serves: 4**

Ingredients:

2 large eggs
Salt & pepper
6 English sausages
4 large mushrooms
1 teaspoon butter
6 bacon
2 large tomatoes
200g baked beans

Preparation:

1. Grease two ramekins with butter and crack eggs. 2. Place the ramekins in the air fryer basket along with bacon, sausages, tomatoes and mushrooms. 3. Season mushrooms and tomatoes with salt and pepper. 4. Cook for 5 minutes in 180°C. Remove eggs from the air fryer. Cook the rest for another 5 minutes. 5. Dish out and serve warm with canned beans.

Serving Suggestions: Serve with toast and English tea.
Variation Tip: You can also do scrambled eggs.
Nutritional Information per Serving: Calories: 149 | Fat: 124g | Sat Fat: 42g | Carbohydrates: 22 g | Fiber: 6g | Sugar: 4g | Protein: 70g

Mini Cheese Chorizo Frittatas

⏱ **Prep Time: 8 minutes**   🍲 **Cook: 20 minutes**   ❧ **Serves: 8**

Ingredients:

140g potatoes
6 eggs, beaten
115g chorizo diced
Salt and pepper for seasoning
85g frozen peas, defrosted
Few sprigs of parsley, finely chopped
55g cheddar, grated

Preparation:

1. Boil potatoes for 10-15 minutes. Once cooked, drain and set them aside. 2. Cut the potatoes into slices. 3. Switch the air fryer to 200°C and preheat for 10 minutes. 4. Line a muffin tray that fits in the air fryer with muffin liners. 5. In a bowl, add eggs, peas, parsley, and chorizo. Season with salt and pepper. 5. Line the muffin tray with potato slices and spoon out the egg mixture. Top with cheese and place the muffin tray in the air fryer. Cook for 15-20 minutes until frittatas are firm and lightly browned. 6. Serve warm.

Serving Suggestions: You can serve it with sweet Thai chili sauce.
Variation Tip: You can serve it with tartar sauce too.
Nutritional Information per Serving: Calories: 172 | Fat: 11g | Sat Fat: 4g | Carbohydrates: 5g | Fiber: 1g | Sugar: 0g | Protein: 12g

Bacon Butty Sandwich

⏱ **Prep Time: 5 minutes**   🍽 **Cook: 7 minutes**   🥩 **Serves: 1**

Ingredients:

2 slices bacon
2 slices of farmhouse bread
½ teaspoon butter
¼ teaspoon HP steak sauce
¼ teaspoon Worcestershire sauce

Preparation:

1. Preheat Air fryer at 175°C for 7 minutes. 2. Place bacon strips in the basket and cook for 4 minutes. Once done, remove from the air fryer. 3. Next place bread slices in the air fryer in a single layer and cook for 3 minutes. 4. Remove from the air fryer once it is lightly brown and crisp. 5. Assemble Bacon Butty by smearing butter on the slices. Next place bacon strips and drizzle Hp sauce and Worcestershire sauce. Place the other slice on top. 6. Serve immediately.
Serving Suggestions: Serve with favorite dipping sauce.
Variation Tip: You can use turkey bacon.
Nutritional Information per Serving: Calories: 169 | Fat: 6.4g | Sat Fat: 2.2g | Carbohydrates: 22.9g | Fiber: 1.3g | Sugar: 4.3g | Protein: 5.1g

Cloud Eggs on Toast

⏱ **Prep Time: 10 minutes**   🍽 **Cook: 13 minutes**   🥩 **Serves: 2**

Ingredients:

2 large eggs
2 tablespoons chives, chopped
Slices of sour dough bread

Preparation:

1. Switch the air-fryer at 175°C. 2. Separate egg yolks and white. 3. Whisk egg whites with the electric beater until stiff peaks. 4. Place parchment paper on an air fryer tray and then scoop out a large dollop of egg white on the parchment paper. 5. Place the tray in the air fryer for 8 minutes until it turns light golden. 6. Gently place an egg yolk on top of the baked egg whites. Cook in the air fryer for another 2 minutes. 7. Place carefully on the toast and garnish chopped chives. 8. Serve warm.
Serving Suggestions: Serve with baked beans
Variation Tip: You can also serve with sausages on the side as well.
Nutritional Information per Serving: Calories: 80 | Fat: 6g | Sat Fat: 2g | Carbohydrates: 0.3g | Fiber: 0.3g | Sugar: 0.3g | Protein: 7g

Pumpkin Scones

⏱ **Prep Time: 15 minutes**   🍽 **Cook: 12 minutes**   🥩 **Serves: 6**

Ingredients:

375g self-raising flour, plus extra for rolling
50g caster sugar
115g cold butter
240g cooked pumpkin
1-2 tsp pumpkin spice
60ml milk

Preparation:

1. Switch the air fryer to 200°C and preheat for 10 minutes. 2. Mix butter, flour, sugar and pumpkin spice to form a coarse mixture. 3. Add cooked pumpkin and milk and knead the dough. If the dough is hard, you can add more milk. 4. Roll the dough and cut triangles or circles. Roll the trimmings again and repeat the same steps until all the dough is utilized. 5. Brush with the milk and place in the air fryer. Cook for 10-12 minutes until lightly brown. 6. Cook the rest of the scones in batches. 7. Dish out and serve.
Serving Suggestions: Serve with butter or cream cheese flavored frosting with a pinch of cinnamon, to serve
Variation Tip: You can use caramel topping as well.
Nutritional Information per Serving: Calories: 414 | Fat: 16.3g | Sat Fat: 10g | Carbohydrates: 60g | Fiber: 2.9g | Sugar: 10.3g | Protein: 7.4g

Walnut Banana Muffins

🕑 **Prep Time: 15 minutes** 🍲 **Cook: 25 minutes** 🍃 **Serves: 8**

Ingredients:

1 pinch of salt
2 ripe bananas, peeled and mashed
1 egg
50g brown sugar
½ teaspoon vanilla essence
1½ tablespoon milk
2 tablespoons Nutella
30g walnuts
Dry Ingredients:
190g plain flour
½ teaspoon baking soda
½ teaspoon baking powder
¼ teaspoon ground cinnamon

Preparation:

1. Mix dry ingredients by sifting the flour, baking soda, baking powder, cinnamon, and salt. 2. Mix the remaining ingredients in another bowl except for the walnuts. 3. Add the banana mixture until just combined. 4. Fold in the walnuts. 5. Switch the Air Fryer to 120°C. Grease a muffin mold that fits in the air fryer. 6. Put the mixture evenly into the prepared muffin molds. 7. Air Fry for about 20 minutes. Check by inserting a toothpick, it should come out clean. 8. Remove the muffin molds from Air Fryer and let them cool for 10 minutes. 9. Serve.
Serving Suggestions: Serve with cream cheese.
Variation Tip: You can use chopped pecans instead of walnuts.
Nutritional Information per Serving: Calories: 223 | Fat: 9g | Sat Fat: 4g | Carbohydrates: 30g | Fiber: 1g | Sugar: 13g | Protein: 4g

Scrambled Eggs with Tomatoes

🕑 **Prep Time: 15 minutes** 🍲 **Cook: 11 minutes** 🍃 **Serves: 4**

Ingredients:

4 eggs
180ml milk
Salt and freshly ground black pepper
8 cherry tomatoes, halved
50g Parmesan cheese, grated

Preparation:

1. Switch the air-fryer to 180°C. Grease an Air Fryer pan with cooking spray. Mix the milk, eggs, salt, and black pepper in a bowl. 2. Transfer the egg mixture to the prepared pan. 3. Air Fry for about 6 minutes until the edges begin to set. 4. With a wooden spatula, stir the egg mixture. 5. Top with the tomatoes and air fry for about 3 minutes or until the eggs are done. 6. Toast a slice of bread in the air-fryer for 2 minutes at 175°C. 7. Place the scrambled eggs with tomatoes on the bread. Serve warm and garnish with parmesan cheese.
Serving Suggestions: Serve with tea
Variation Tip: You can top it with cheddar cheese instead of parmesan
Nutritional Information per Serving: Calories: 341 | Fat: 17g | Sat Fat: 1g | Carbohydrates: 25.2g | Fiber: 1.2g | Sugar: 17.7g | Protein: 26.4g

Orange Blueberry Muffins

⏰ Prep Time: 15 minutes 🍲 Cook: 12 minutes 🍽 Serves: 12

Ingredients:

265g self-raising flour
100g white sugar
120ml milk
1 teaspoon vanilla extract
57g butter, melted
2 eggs
2 teaspoons fresh orange zest, finely grated
2 tablespoons fresh orange juice
75g fresh blueberries

Preparation:

1. Switch the Air Fryer to 180°C. Grease a muffin pan. 2. Mix flour and white sugar in a bowl. 3. In another large bowl, mix well the remaining ingredients except for the blueberries. 4. Now, add in the flour mixture and mix until just combined. Then fold in the blueberries. 5. Put the mixture evenly into the prepared muffin molds. Arrange the molds into the Air Fryer. 6. Air Fry for 12 minutes. 7. Remove the muffin molds from Air Fryer and let them cool for about 10 minutes. 8. Carefully invert the muffins onto the wire rack to cool completely before serving. 9. Serve.

Serving Suggestions: Serve with coffee
Variation Tip: You can top it with blueberry sauce and buttercream.
Nutritional Information per Serving: Calories: 154 | Fat: 5g | Sat Fat: 1g | Carbohydrates: 23.7g | Fiber: 1g | Sugar: 6.4g | Protein: 3.7g

Caramel Chocolate Crumpets with Peanut Praline

⏰ Prep Time: 5 minutes 🍲 Cook: 18 minutes 🍽 Serves: 2

Ingredients:

12 Golden Crumpets
50g caster sugar
2 tablespoons salted peanuts
Pinch of salt
40g dark chocolate, chopped
80ml caramel sauce
85g peanut butter
2 tablespoons light cream

Preparation:

1. Switch the air fryer to 200°C. 2. Place baking paper in the air fryer tray and put peanuts. Air fryer to 3 minutes and remove from the air fryer. 3. For peanut praline: In a pan, dissolve sugar with 2 tablespoons of water on low heat until brown. Pour over roasted peanuts and set aside to cool. 4. Combine caramel with salt. 5. In a saucepan, heat the chocolate and cream and cook for 4 minutes until the chocolate is melted. 6. Switch the air fryer to 85°C and place the crumpets in the air fryer for 2 minutes. 7. Serve the crumpets on a plate, spread peanut butter, and place another crumpet over it, drizzle salted caramel sauce over it. Stack another crumpet and drizzle chocolate sauce, coarsely chop peanut praline and sprinkle over the crumpets. Make stacks of crumpets in the same manner. 8. Finally, top with fresh whipped cream.

Serving Suggestions: Serve with blueberries.
Variation Tip: You can also top it with cream cheese as well.
Nutritional Information per Serving: Calories:604 | Fat: 24.9g | Sat Fat: 7.5g | Carbohydrates: 83.4g | Fiber: 4.9g | Sugar: 22.6g | Protein: 16.3g

Creamy Fried Squid and Egg Yolks

⏰ **Prep Time: 15 minutes**   🍲 **Cook: 20 minutes**   🍃 **Serves: 4**

Ingredients:

65g self-raising flour
400g squid, cleaned and pat dried
Salt and freshly ground black pepper
1 tablespoon olive oil
2 tablespoons butter
2 green chilies, seeded and chopped
2 curry leaves stalks
4 raw egg yolks
120ml chicken broth
2 tablespoons evaporated milk
1 tablespoon sugar

Preparation:

1. Switch the Air Fryer to 180°C. Grease an Air Fryer pan. 2. Sprinkle the squid flower evenly with salt and black pepper. 3. In a shallow dish, add the flour. Coat the squid evenly with flour and then shake off any excess flour. 4. Place the squid into the prepared pan in a single layer. 5. Air Fry for about 9 minutes. 6. Remove from the Air Fryer and set aside. 7. In a skillet heat butter and sauté the chilies and curry leaves for about 3 minutes. 8. Add the egg yolks and cook for about 1 minute, stirring continuously. 9. Gradually, add the chicken broth and cook for about 3-5 minutes, stirring continuously. 10. Add in the milk and sugar and mix until well combined. 11. Add the fried squid and toss to coat well. 12. Serve hot.

Serving Suggestions: Serve with crusted bread
Variation Tip: You can add coconut milk.
Nutritional Information per Serving: Calories: 311 | Fat: 16.1g | Sat Fat: 1.3g | Carbohydrates: 19.8g | Fiber: 13.7g | Sugar: 4.2g | Protein: 21g

Breakfast Yoghurt Carrot Muffins

⏰ **Prep Time: 15 minutes**   🍲 **Cook: 12 minutes**   🍃 **Serves: 6**

Ingredients:

120ml yoghurt
1 teaspoon vinegar
1 tablespoon vegetable oil
3 tablespoons cottage cheese, grated
1 carrot, peeled and grated
2-4 tablespoons water (if needed)
For Muffins:
30g whole-wheat flour
30g plain flour
½ teaspoon baking powder
⅛ teaspoon baking soda
½ teaspoon dried parsley, crushed
½ teaspoon salt

Preparation:

1. Switch the Air Fryer to 180°C. Grease 6 medium muffin molds. 2. For muffins: Mix flour, baking powder, baking soda, parsley, and salt in a bowl. Mix well the yoghurt, and vinegar along with the rest of the ingredients. 3. Place the mixture evenly into the prepared muffin molds. 4. Place the muffin molds into an Air Fryer in 2 batches. 5. Air Fry for about 12 minutes. Check by inserting a skewer. It should come out clean. 6. Remove the muffin molds from Air Fryer and let them cool for 10 minutes. 7. Carefully, invert the muffins onto the wire rack to completely cool before serving. 8. Enjoy!

Serving Suggestions: Serve by topping with sesame seeds
Variation Tip: You can add walnuts as well.
Nutritional Information per Serving: Calories: 222 | Fat: 12.9g | Sat Fat: 5.7g | Carbohydrates: 12.4g | Fiber: 0.9g | Sugar: 2.2g | Protein: 15.1g

Chocolate Chip Banana Bread

⏱ **Prep Time: 6 minutes**   🍲 **Cook: 20 minutes**   ❧ **Serves: 10**

❱ Ingredients:

250g plain flour
½ teaspoon baking soda
½ teaspoon baking powder
½ teaspoon salt
150g sugar
75g butter, softened

3 eggs
1 tablespoon vanilla extract
240ml milk
120g bananas, peeled and mashed
175g chocolate chips

❱ Preparation:

1. Dump in flour, baking powder, salt and baking soda and mix well. Beat sugar and butter until creamy. 2. Beat in eggs, and vanilla extract. Then, add the flour mixture and mix until well combined. 3. Add in the milk, and mashed bananas and mix them. Gently, fold in the chocolate chips. 4. Switch the Air Fryer to 180°C. 5. Grease a loaf pan and Pour the mixture into the prepared pan. 6. Arrange the loaf pan into an Air Fryer basket. 7. Air Fry for about 20 minutes. 8. Remove from Air Fryer once cooked and let it cool for 10 minutes. 9. Cut the bread into desired size slices and serve.
Serving Suggestions: Serve with butter.
Variation Tip: You can add nuts and raisins as well.
Nutritional Information per Serving: Calories: 333 | Fat: 13.2g | Sat Fat: 8.1g | Carbohydrates: 47.4g | Fiber: 1.5g | Sugar: 26g | Protein: 6.5g

Eggy Bread

⏱ **Prep Time: 5 minutes**   🍲 **Cook: 10 minutes**   ❧ **Serves: 2**

❱ Ingredients:

2 slices white bread or brown bread
2 medium eggs
1 tablespoon milk
1 tablespoon melted butter
Oil spray
Cinnamon sugar for topping (¼ teaspoon cinnamon plus 2 teaspoons of caster sugar)

❱ Preparation:

1. Mix the eggs, milk, and butter and whisk well. 2. Dip the bread pieces in the mixture. 3. Switch the air-fryer at 160°C and preheat for 10 minutes. 4. Spray the basket with cooking spray and place the soaked bread pieces in a single layer. 5. Cook for 6 minutes, flipping halfway through to the cook time. 6. Sprinkle cinnamon sugar on top. 7. Serve warm.
Serving Suggestions: Serve with maple butter.
Variation Tip: You can also serve it with custard.
Nutritional Information per Serving: Calories: 288 | Fat: 21.7g | Sat Fat: 10.4g | Carbohydrates: 10.6g | Fiber: 0.4g | Sugar: 2.2g | Protein: 13.1g

Scrambled Egg with Mushrooms

⏱ **Prep Time: 15 minutes**   🍲 **Cook: 10 minutes**   ❧ **Serves: 2**

❱ Ingredients:

4 eggs
75g fresh mushrooms, finely chopped
2 tablespoons unsalted butter
2 tablespoons Parmesan cheese, shredded
A pinch of salt and black pepper, to taste

❱ Preparation:

1. Switch the Air Fryer to 140°C. 2. Mix the eggs, salt, and black pepper in a bowl. 3. Grease the pan with butter. 4. Add the beaten eggs and Air Fry for about 4-5 minutes. 5. Add in the mushrooms and cook for 5 minutes, stirring occasionally. 6. Serve hot.
Serving Suggestions: Serve with parmesan cheese
Variation Tip: You can add chopped onions and bell peppers for taste variations
Nutritional Information per Serving: Calories: 254 | Fat: 11g | Sat Fat: 1.1g | Carbohydrates: 2.1g | Fiber: 13.7g | Sugar: 1.4g | Protein: 12.8g

Scottish Oats Porridge with Blueberries

⏰ Prep Time: 5 minutes   🍲 Cook: 5 minutes   ❧ Serves: 2

Ingredients:

45g rolled oats
240ml whole milk
2 tablespoons Blueberry sauce
Pinch of salt
Fresh Blueberries for garnishing

Preparation:

1. Switch the air-fryer at 95°C and begin preheating. 2. In a small bowl that fits the air-fryer basket, add oats and the rest of the ingredients except for fresh blueberries. 3. Mix and put in the air-fryer for 3 minutes. Stir and change the side of the bowl and cook again for 2 more minutes. 4. Serve warm and garnish with blueberries.
Serving Suggestions: You can drizzle blueberry sauce and nuts.
Variation Tip: You can use plant based milk instead of whole milk.
Nutritional Information per Serving: Calories: 301 | Fat: 10.6g | Sat Fat: 5g | Carbohydrates: 38.7g | Fiber: 4.1g | Sugar: 13.2g | Protein: 13.2g

English Breakfast Potato Frittata

⏰ Prep Time: 10 minutes   🍲 Cook: 25 minutes   ❧ Serves: 4

Ingredients:

8 large eggs
310g potato slices
2 tablespoons olive oil
6 bacon slices, chopped
Bunch of spring onions, sliced
12 cherry tomatoes
Salt and black pepper, to taste
Handful grated Cheddar

Preparation:

1. Switch the air fryer to 200°C and preheat for 10 minutes. 2. Boil potatoes for 4 minutes on medium heat. Once cooked, drain and spread on a tea towel. 3. When they are slightly cooled, spray them with oil and pop them in the air fryer for 5 minutes. Remove once they are brown from the edges. 4. Next, add bacon slices in the air fryer and cook for 5 minutes. 5. In a baking dish, place potatoes and bacon. Add spring onions and cherry tomatoes. 6. Whisk eggs with salt and pepper and pour over the potatoes. Cover with grated cheddar cheese. 7. Pop the dish back and air fry for 7 minutes until the cheese melts and the eggs are cooked. 8. If your air fryer has a grill function, then place it under the grill for 5 minutes to set and brown the top.
Serving Suggestions: Serve with toast and relish
Variation Tip: You can also add black pudding and mushrooms.
Nutritional Information per Serving: Calories: 539 | Fat: g | Sat Fat: 14.1g | Carbohydrates: 16.2 g | Fiber: 4.5g | Sugar: 10.7g | Protein: 33.5g

Chapter 2 Snack and Starter Recipes

Sweet Potato Chips

⏲ **Prep Time: 5 minutes   Cook time: 15 minutes   Serves: 2**

Ingredients:

Cooking oil spray (coconut, sunflower, or safflower)
1 small-medium sweet potato, unpeeled, thinly sliced
¼ teaspoon dried rosemary
Dash sea salt

Preparation:

1. Spray the air fryer basket with oil. 2. Place the sweet potato slices in the basket, spreading them out as much as possible, and spray the tops with oil. 3. Air-fry the slices at 200°C for 12 minutes; spray them with oil and sprinkle them with rosemary and sea salt after 4 minutes; flip them and spray them with oil one more time when there are 4 minutes of cooking time left. 4. You can let them crisp up at room temperature after cooking. 5. Serve warm.

Serving Suggestions: Enjoy with a light garlic aioli or a sprinkle of smoked paprika for extra flavor.

Variation Tip: Swap rosemary with thyme or cinnamon for a different flavor profile.

Nutritional Information per Serving: Calories: 58 | Fat: 0.1g | Sat Fat: 0g | Carbohydrates: 13.4g | Fiber: 1.9g | Sugar: 4.3g | Protein: 1.0g

Parmesan Courgette Chips

⏲ **Prep Time: 5 minutes   Cook time: 25 minutes   Serves: 2**

Ingredients:

3 medium courgette, sliced
1 teaspoon parsley, chopped
3 tablespoon parmesan cheese, grated
Pepper to taste
Salt to taste

Preparation:

1. Preheat the air fryer at 220°C. 2. Put the sliced courgette on a sheet of baking paper and spritz with cooking spray. 3. Combine the cheese, pepper, parsley, and salt, and then top the sliced courgette with the cheese mixture. 4. Air-fry the food for 25 minutes until crisp. 5. Serve hot.

Serving Suggestions: Serve as a side dish or enjoy as a healthy snack with a marinara or garlic yogurt dip.

Variation Tip: Add a sprinkle of chili flakes to the cheese mixture for a spicy kick.

Nutritional Information per Serving: Calories: 38 | Fat: 2.2g | Sat Fat: 1.3g | Carbohydrates: 2.3g | Fiber: 0.5g | Sugar: 0.02g | Protein: 2.7g

Crispy White Mushrooms

⏰ **Prep Time: 10 minutes   Cook time: 10 minutes   Serves: 2**

Ingredients:

75g gluten-free crispy rice cereal
1 teaspoon Italian seasoning
1 teaspoon nutritional yeast
⅛ teaspoon salt
1 tablespoon Dijon mustard
1 tablespoon vegan mayonnaise
60ml plain unsweetened almond milk
200g whole white mushrooms

Preparation:

1. Add the cereal, Italian seasoning, nutritional yeast, and salt to a food processor, and then pulse them until a bread crumb consistency forms. 2. Whisk the mustard, mayonnaise, and almond milk in a bowl. 3. Preheat the air fryer at 175°C for 3 minutes. 4. Dip mushrooms in wet mixture, and shake off any excess. Dredge them in dry mixture, and shake off any excess. 5. Lightly grease the air fryer basket with cooking oil, and then arrange the mushrooms into the air fryer basket. 6. Air-fry the mushrooms for 7 minutes, tossing them halfway through. 7. Serve warm.

Serving Suggestions: Pair with a tangy vegan ranch or marinara sauce for dipping.
Variation Tip: Substitute white mushrooms with button or cremini mushrooms for added flavor.
Nutritional Information per Serving: Calories: 197 | Fat: 4.3g | Sat Fat: 0.6g | Carbohydrates: 35.7g | Fiber: 4.2g | Sugar: 6.7g | Protein: 6.5g

Simple French Fries

⏰ **Prep Time: 5 minutes   Cook time: 25 minutes   Serves: 3**

Ingredients:

2 medium potatoes, preferably Yukon Gold (but any kind will do)
Cooking oil spray (sunflower, safflower, or refined coconut)
2 teaspoons oil (olive, sunflower, or melted coconut)
½ teaspoon garlic granules
¼ teaspoon plus ⅛ teaspoon sea salt
¼ teaspoon freshly ground black pepper
¼ teaspoon paprika
Ketchup, hot sauce, for serving

Preparation:

1. Scrub the potatoes and cut them into ½ cm thick. 2. Toss the cut potato pieces with the oil, garlic, salt, pepper, and paprika in a bowl. 3. Spray the air fryer basket with oil, and place the potato pieces in it; air-fry the potato pieces at 200°C for 22 minutes until they are tender and nicely browned, stirring them every 8 minutes. 4. Serve the fries with the sauce of your choice.

Serving Suggestions: Serve with ketchup, hot sauce, or a light garlic aioli for dipping.
Variation Tip: Add fresh herbs like rosemary or thyme to the seasoning for a fragrant twist.
Nutritional Information per Serving: Calories: 218 | Fat: 3.3g | Sat Fat: 0.5g | Carbohydrates: 43.4g | Fiber: 5.5g | Sugar: 2.0g | Protein: 5.1g

Crispy Potatoes and Asparagus

⏱ **Prep Time: 10 minutes** 🍲 **Cook: 30 minutes** 🍃 **Serves: 6**

Ingredients:

680g Baby Potatoes, quartered
225g Asparagus
2 tablespoons Olive Oil, divided
2 tablespoons Rosemary Leaves, roughly chopped
2 teaspoon Garlic Powder
½ teaspoon Black Pepper
¼-½ teaspoon Red Pepper Flakes
Pinch of Kosher Salt

Preparation:

1. Switch the air fryer to 200°C. 2. Spray oil on the potatoes and season with salt and pepper. Air fry for 15-20 minutes until tender. Shake halfway through the cooking time. 3. In a bowl toss asparagus and rosemary in oil and season with garlic powder, salt, pepper and red chili flakes. 4. Add roasted potatoes and asparagus and toss them together. 5. Pop it again in the air fryer for 6-8 minutes until asparagus is crisp. 6. Dish out and serve.

Serving Suggestions: Serve with yoghurt dip.
Variation Tip: You can serve with Grated Parmesan and Fresh Lemon Wedges.
Nutritional Information per Serving: Calories: 444 | Fat: 8g | Sat Fat: 1.3g | Carbohydrates: 82.1g | Fiber: 17.7g | Sugar: 1.4g | Protein: 17.6g

Cheesy Beans On Toast

⏱ **Prep Time: 10 minutes** 🍲 **Cook: 25 minutes** 🍃 **Serves: 6**

Ingredients:

2 tablespoons olive oil
2 teaspoon dried oregano
1 onion, finely chopped
1 garlic clove, crushed
400g can chopped tomatoes
400g can cannellini beans, drained
1 tablespoon tomato purée
Salt and black pepper, to taste
115g mozzarella cheese shredded
4 large slices sourdough bread
Sliced pepperoni

Preparation:

1. Heat oil and fry the onions until softened. Add oregano and garlic, then add in the tomato purée, tomatoes and season it with salt and pepper. 2. Let it simmer for 10 minutes. Remove from heat and blend everything with the stick blender. Stir in the beans and put it back on the heat for 5 more minutes. 3. Switch the air fryer at 150°C. Toast the bread slices in the air fryer for 3 minutes until lightly toasted. 4. Flip the bread and top each toast with the bean mixture, mozzarella cheese, and pepperoni slices. 5. Cook in the air fryer for 3 more minutes or until the cheese has melted. Serve warm.

Serving Suggestions: You can serve with greens of your choice.
Variation Tip: you can use ham slices and basil leaves for garnishing.
Nutritional Information per Serving: Calories: 578 | Fat: 15g | Sat Fat: 6g | Carbohydrates: 78g | Fiber: 12g | Sugar: 0g | Protein: 27g

Cheesy Hash Brown Casserole

⏰ Prep Time: 10 minutes 🍲 Cook: 10 minutes 🍃 Serves: 2

Ingredients:

2 eggs
1 large potato, coarsely grated
1 tablespoon plain flour
3 spring onions, finely sliced
4 tablespoons cheddar, grated
1 tablespoon vegetable oil

Preparation:

1. Switch the air fryer to 175°C. 2. Drain all the water from the potatoes. 3. Whisk eggs and add potatoes, flour, cheese, and sliced spring onions. Season generously with salt and pepper. 4. Grease a small heat proof dish with oil and add potato mixture. Cook in the air fryer for 7 minutes. 5. Spread remaining grated cheese on the top and cook for another 3-4 minutes or until the cheese has been melted. 6. Serve Warm.

Serving Suggestions: Serve by garnishing dried parsley or chili flakes.

Variation Tip: You can also use sausage meat for taste variation.

Nutritional Information per Serving: Calories: 661 | Fat: 35g | Sat Fat: 12g | Carbohydrates: 54g | Fiber: 5g | Sugar: 0g | Protein: 30g

Chocolate Pear Flapjacks

⏰ Prep Time: 10 minutes 🍲 Cook: 15 minutes 🍃 Serves: 4

Ingredients:

310g porridge oats
4 tablespoon honey
140g butter, plus a little extra for the tin
140g light brown soft sugar
115g dark chocolate, melted
4 pear halves drained from a can

Preparation:

1. Switch the air fryer at 175°C and preheat for 10 minutes. 2. Grease a pan that fits in the air fryer. 3. In a saucepan melt butter, brown sugar and honey. Once melted, take it off from the heat. 4. Dice pears into small chunks. 5. Fold out and pears in the butter mixture. Mix well to combine. 6. Add the mixture in the greased pan and press with the back of the spoon. 7. Place in the microwave and cook for 10 minutes. 8. Prepare topping: Microwave chocolate for 20 seconds, stir and then microwave again for 15 seconds. 9. Once the flapjacks are done, remove them from the air fryer. Cut squares and drizzle melted chocolate once flapjacks are cooled down. 10. Serve.

Serving Suggestions: Serve with tea.

Variation Tip: You can use hazelnuts or pecans as well.

Nutritional Information per Serving: Calories: 320 | Fat: 16g | Sat Fat: 9g | Carbohydrates: 39g | Fiber: 3g | Sugar: 0g | Protein: 4g

Lemon Cream Scones

🕐 **Prep Time:** 10 minutes 🍲 **Cook:** 12 minutes 🍃 **Serves:** 10

Ingredients:

340g self-raising flour, plus extra for dusting
1 tablespoon baking powder
120ml lemonade
50g caster sugar
120ml double cream
1 egg, beaten

Preparation:

1. Switch the air-fryer at 200°C and preheat for 10 minutes. 2. Mix sugar, flour and baking powder in a bowl. 3. Pour cream and lemonade in the flour mixture and knead to a soft dough. 4. Roll the dough to 2cm-thickness and cut circles with the cookie cutter. 5. Brush the top of the scones with beaten egg and place scones in the air fryer for 12 minutes. Cook the rest in batches. 6. Serve with tea.
Serving Suggestions: Serve with butter and marmalade
Variation Tip: You can add butter instead of double cream.
Nutritional Information per Serving: Calories: 217 | Fat: 7g | Sat Fat: 4g | Carbohydrates: 33g | Fiber: 1g | Sugar: 4g | Protein: 17g

Cheesy Apple and Potato Pasties

🕐 **Prep Time:** 30 minutes 🍲 **Cook:** 25 minutes 🍃 **Serves:** 6

Ingredients:

310g cold butter
500g all-purpose flour, plus extra for dusting
50g caster sugar (optional)
Salt and pepper for seasoning

2 medium potatoes, boiled and cubed
3 Granny Smith apples, peeled and cubed
340g hard cheese, grated
Milk for brushing the pasties

Preparation:

1. Switch the air fryer at 175°C and preheat for 10 minutes. 2. Mix flour, salt, pepper and butter to form a crumbly texture. Add some cold water to form a firm dough. Cover and let it rest for 20 minutes. 3. For the Filling: Mix potatoes, cheese, apples, sugar and season with salt and pepper. 4. Make six balls out of the dough and roll out. Place in the pastry dough, add a tablespoon of filling and close the mold to shape the pasty. 5. Brush milk on the pasties and place in the air fryer. 6. Cook for 25 minutes and remove once they are golden brown in color. 7. Repeat the same steps for the remaining batches.
Serving Suggestions: Serve with cream cheese.
Variation Tip: You can use Lincolnshire Poacher or Cornish cheddar work well too.
Nutritional Information per Serving: Calories: 188 | Fat: 14g | Sat Fat: 3g | Carbohydrates: 10g | Fiber: 1g | Sugar: 1g | Protein: 7g

Cinnamon Apple Crisps

🕐 **Prep Time:** 5 minutes 🍲 **Cook:** 30 minutes 🍃 **Serves:** 4

Ingredients:

2 Granny Smiths
Cinnamon, for sprinkling

Preparation:

1. Switch the air-fryer at 175°C. 2. Core and slice apples through the equator into very thin slices. 3. Line the apples in a single layer and cook for 30 minutes until crisp and golden. 4. Cook all the batches in the same way and remove in a large bowl. 5. Sprinkle cinnamon and toss carefully.
Serving Suggestions: Serve topped with lemon wedges.
Variation Tip: You can skip nutmeg for taste variation.
Nutritional Information per Serving: Calories: 90 | Fat: 0.3g | Sat Fat: 0g | Carbohydrates: 22g | Fiber: 3.3g | Sugar: 22g | Protein:0.8g

Mini Crumpets Pizza

🕑 **Prep Time: 20 minutes**   🍲 **Cook: 5 minutes**   🍃 **Serves: 6**

) Ingredients:

6 crumpets
4 tablespoons passata
4 tablespoons ketchup
½ teaspoon dried oregano
Peppers, cherry tomatoes, red onion, olives, ham and basil-chopped in small pieces for the topping
85g cheddar cheese, grated

) Preparation:

1. Switch the air fryer at 175°C and lightly toast the crumpets. 2. Mix passata, ketchup and oregano together. 3. Spread sauce over the crumpets, followed by chopped vegetables and top with grated cheese. 4. Place the crumpets in the air fryer tray and cook for 3-4 minutes until the cheese has melted and turned golden. 5. Dish out and serve right away.
Serving Suggestions: Serve with ketchup and garnish with chopped parsley
Variation Tip: You can also use pepperoni slices.
Nutritional Information per Serving: Calories: 145 | Fat: 5g | Sat Fat: 3g | Carbohydrates: 18g | Fiber: 1g | Sugar: 2g | Protein: 6g

Golden Prawn Balls

🕑 **Prep Time: 45 minutes**   🍲 **Cook: 6 minutes**   🍃 **Serves: 6**

) Ingredients:

255g thawed prawn meat, cleaned and deveined
1 teaspoon olive oil, plus extra, to brush
1 green shallot, very thinly sliced
1 teaspoon ginger, finely grated
2 garlic cloves, finely chopped
1 egg white
½ teaspoon caster sugar
2 teaspoon soy sauce
140g sesame seeds, lightly toasted
2 eggs, lightly whisked
Bread crumbs for coating

) Preparation:

1. Switch the air-fryer to 75°C and preheat for 10 minutes. 2. In a food processor add prawns, sugar, garlic, ginger, soya sauce, sugar, egg white, oil and sesame seeds. Process until a paste like consistency forms. Fold chopped shallots and place the mixture in the fridge for 30 minutes. 3. In two separate bowls, place eggs and bread crumbs. Take one tablespoon of the mixture and roll into a ball. Dunk in egg and coat breadcrumbs. 4. Air fry for 6 minutes or until golden. Cook the remaining prawn balls in the same manner. 5. Serve warm and enjoy.
Serving Suggestions: Serve with honey mustard sauce
Variation Tip: You can spice it up by using cayenne pepper.
Nutritional Information per Serving: Calories: 198 | Fat: 14g | Sat Fat: 2.2g | Carbohydrates: 7g | Fiber: 2.9g | Sugar: 0.6g | Protein: 12.8g

Crispy Honey Mustard Halloumi Bars

⏰ **Prep Time: 20 minutes** 🍽 **Cook: 10 minutes** 🍃 **Serves: 8**

> **Ingredients:**

450g haloumi, cut in 1cm wide batons
2 teaspoons Mustard Powder
30g plain flour
1 egg, lightly whisked
100g panko breadcrumbs
Honey Mustard Mayo:
120ml mayonnaise
60ml thickened cream
1 tablespoon honey
2 teaspoons Mustard Powder

> **Preparation:**

1. Switch the air-fryer to 200°C and preheat for 10 minutes. 2. Prepare sauce: Combine all the honey mustard sauce ingredients and mix well. 3. Prepare coating by combining flour and mustard powder. 4. Lightly whisk egg in a separate bowl and keep panko bread crumbs in a shallow container. 5. Coat haloumi in flour mixture, then dunk in egg and finally coat bread crumbs. 6. Air fry haloumi for 10 minutes until crisped and golden. 7. Cook the other batch in the same manner. 8. Dish out and serve.

Serving Suggestions: Serve with your favorite dipping sauce.
Variation Tip: You can also use your favorite seasoning mix in the flour mixture.
Nutritional Information per Serving: Calories: 213 | Fat: 17g | Sat Fat: 6g | Carbohydrates: 5g | Fiber: 1g | Sugar: 1g | Protein: 9g

Puff Pastry Pigs in a Blanket

⏰ **Prep Time: 10 minutes** 🍽 **Cook: 25 minutes** 🍃 **Serves: 8**

> **Ingredients:**

155g ready-rolled puff pastry
16 pork chipolatas
½ tablespoon vegetable oil, for greasing
1 egg yolk, beaten, to glaze

> **Preparation:**

1. Switch the air-fryer to 80°C and preheat for 5 minutes. 2. Grease the air fryer sheet pan with oil. 3. Cut 16 strips from the puff pastry. Each should be 10 cm-long. 4. Wrap around chipolatas and place in the fridge for 15 minutes. 5. Once chilled, brush them with beaten egg yolk and air fry for 25 minutes. 6. Cook until the pastry is puffed and golden brown remove from the air fryer. Cook other batches in the same manner. 7. Serve and Enjoy!

Serving Suggestions: Serve with your favorite dip.
Variation Tip: You can garnish with sesame seeds as well.
Nutritional Information per Serving: Calories: 205 | Fat: 15g | Sat Fat: 6g | Carbohydrates: 9g | Fiber: 1g | Sugar: 1g | Protein: 8g

Grilled Courgette Cheese Rolls

⏰ **Prep Time:** 15 minutes   🍲 **Cook:** 5 minutes   ❧ **Serves:** 8

Ingredients:

2 medium courgette, thinly sliced lengthways
85g soft goat's cheese
3 teaspoon milk
Salt and pepper for seasoning
1 tablespoon finely chopped fresh mint leaves
Olive oil cooking spray

Preparation:

1. Spray a grill pan with oil. Chargrill courgette slices for 1-2 minutes, each side. Transfer onto a plate and set aside to cool. 2. For the filling: Combine mint, cheese, and milk in a small bowl. Season with salt and pepper according to your taste. 3. Spread cheese mixture on one side of each courgette slice. 4. Roll up tightly and Secure with a toothpick. 5. Switch the air-fryer to 175°C and place courgette cheese rolls in the air fryer basket for 3 minutes. 6. Dish out and serve.
Serving Suggestions: Garnish it with chopped mint.
Variation Tip: You can use cream instead of milk for the variation in taste.
Nutritional Information per Serving: Calories: 75 | Fat: 4.8g | Sat Fat: 3.2g | Carbohydrates: 3.8g | Fiber: 1.2g | Sugar: 2.1g | Protein: 5.3g

Smoked Salmon and Veggie Quiche Cups

⏰ **Prep Time:** 10 minutes   🍲 **Cook:** 15 minutes   ❧ **Serves:** 6

Ingredients:

310g ready to cook, short crust pastry
2 tablespoons extra-virgin olive oil
Salt and pepper
200g fresh ricotta, crumbled
2 small courgettes, chopped
200g smoked salmon, torn
6 eggs
15g fresh dill sprigs, chopped
15g finely chopped fresh chives
75g peas, thawed
2 tablespoons lemon juice
½ teaspoon of lemon zest
Olive oil for spraying

Preparation:

1. Switch the air-fryer to 175°C and preheat for 10 minutes. 2. Spray oil in the muffin tray. 3. Roll short crust pastry and cut 12 circles with cookie cutter. 4. Mix eggs, peas, ricotta, dill, chives, lemon juice, salmon, courgette and lemon zest in a bowl. Season it with salt and pepper. 5. Divide mixture among muffin tray. Place in the air fryer for 15 minutes or until just set. 6. Cook the next batches in the same way. 7. Serve warm and enjoy.
Serving Suggestions: Serve it with avocado yoghurt dip and garnish it with parsley.
Variation Tip: You can add chili flakes for some heat.
Nutritional Information per Serving: Calories: 620 | Fat: 26.9g | Sat Fat: 7.3g | Carbohydrates: 65.3g | Fiber: 5.5g | Sugar: 10g | Protein: 27g

Crispy Tofu Bites

⏰ **Prep Time: 15 minutes**   **Cook time: 20 minutes**   **Serves: 4**

Ingredients:

For Marinade:

80ml vegetable stock
2 tablespoons tomato sauce
1 tablespoon nutritional yeast
1 teaspoon Italian seasoning
1 teaspoon granulated sugar

½ teaspoon fennel seeds
½ teaspoon garlic powder
¼ teaspoon salt
¼ teaspoon ground black pepper
350g firm tofu, cut into 2 cm cubes

For Breading:

65g plain gluten-free bread crumbs
2 teaspoons nutritional yeast

1 teaspoon Italian seasoning
½ teaspoon salt

For Dip:

240ml marinara sauce, heated

Preparation:

1. Combine all of the marinade ingredients in a large bowl to coat the tofu cubes well. 2. Refrigerate the tofu cubes for 30 minutes, tossing them once after 15 minutes. 3. Preheat the air fryer at 175°C for 3 minutes. 4. Mix up all of the breading ingredients in a shallow dish. 5. Dredge the marinated tofu cubes in bread crumb mixture. 6. Lightly grease the air fryer basket with cooking oil, and then place the tofu cubes in it. 7. Air-fry the tofu cubes for 10 minutes, flipping them and brushing them with additional cooking oil halfway through. You can cook the tofu cubes in batches. 8. Serve warm with marinara dip on the side.

Serving Suggestions: Serve with marinara sauce and a side of steamed veggies.

Variation Tip: Use barbecue sauce or add paprika to the breading for a spicy kick.

Nutritional Information per Serving: Calories: 252 | Fat: 11g | Sat Fat: 1.5g | Carbohydrates: 22g | Fiber: 4g | Sugar: 6g | Protein: 15g

Vegan Shepherd's Pie

⏰ **Prep Time: 10 minutes**   🍲 **Cook: 50 minutes**   🍃 **Serves: 4**

Ingredients:

1 tablespoon olive oil
1 large onion, halved and sliced
455g carrot cubes
2 tablespoon thyme chopped
210ml red wine
300g can chopped tomatoes
2 vegetable stock cubes
300g can of green lentils
900g boiled sweet potatoes
25g butter
75g cheddar, grated

Preparation:

1. In a pan heat oil and sauté onions until golden brown. 2. Add carrots and thyme along with red wine and tomatoes. Stir and add 120 ml of water and vegetable stock cubes. Let it simmer for 10 minutes. 3. Next add lentils and cook for 10 minutes until they become mushy. Dish out in a pie dish that fits in the air fryer. 4. Mash sweet potatoes with butter and mix until smooth. Spread mashed potatoes on top of the vegetables and cover with cheddar cheese. 5. Preheat air fryer to 150°C for 20 minutes. Place the pie dish in the air fryer and cook for 20 minutes until golden brown.

Serving Suggestions: Garnish with coriander and serve with crusted bread.

Variation Tip: You can also use any other vegetables of your choice.

Nutritional Information per Serving: Calories: 540 | Fat: 16g | Sat Fat: 8g | Carbohydrates: 66g | Fiber: 16g | Sugar: 33g | Protein: 16g

Roasted Potatoes

⏱ **Prep Time: 10 minutes**   🍲 **Cook: 15 minutes**   🍃 **Serves: 8**

Ingredients:

1.1kg potatoes, cut in cubes
1 tsp. salt

1 tsp. pepper
50ml oil

Preparation:

1. Parboil potatoes in a large pan. 2. Drain and spread them on a tea towel. 3. Preheat air fryer for 15 minutes at 200°C. 4. Toss the potatoes with oil, salt and pepper. 5. Place them in the air fryer in a single layer and cook for about 15 minutes. Shake them halfway through. 6. Once crisp and golden brown, remove from the air fryer. 7. Serve warm and enjoy.

Serving Suggestions: Serve with Italian seasoning.

Variation Tip: You can garnish Italian basil seasoning for variation in taste.

Nutritional Information per Serving: Calories: 258 | Fat: 11.6g | Sat Fat: 1.5g | Carbohydrates: 35.9g | Fiber: 5.6g | Sugar: 2.6g | Protein: 3.9g

Green Asparagus Soup

⏱ **Prep Time: 10 minutes**   🍲 **Cook: 20 minutes**   🍃 **Serves: 4**

Ingredients:

340g asparagus spears, stalks chopped
2 large handfuls spinach
2 tablespoons butter
3 shallots, finely sliced

Vegetable oil for spraying
2 garlic cloves, crushed
720ml vegetable stock
Salt and pepper for seasoning

Preparation:

1. Switch the air-fryer to 175°C and preheat for 10 minutes. 2. Spray oil on the asparagus stalks and season with salt and pepper. 3. Cook asparagus in the air fryer for 10 minutes. 4. In a pan, heat butter and add garlic and chopped shallots. Sauté for a minute, then add spinach, cooked asparagus, and stock. Let it simmer for 10 minutes. 5. Blend with the stick blender and check for seasoning. 6. Serve piping hot as a side dish, and enjoy.

Serving Suggestions: serve with rustic bread (preferably sourdough)

Variation Tip: You can also top it with salted pumpkin seeds, asparagus tips, and croutons.

Nutritional Information per Serving: Calories: 101 | Fat: 8g | Sat Fat: 4g | Carbohydrates: 4g | Fiber: 4g | Sugar: 4g | Protein: 4g

Creamy Cauliflower Potato Soup

⏱ **Prep Time: 10 minutes**   🍲 **Cook: 2 minutes**   🍃 **Serves: 6**

Ingredients:

450g cauliflower florets
1 medium potato, cut into chunks
60g unsalted butter
1 onion, roughly chopped
480ml whole milk

960ml vegetable stock
60ml double cream
Chopped parsley to serve
Salt and pepper for seasoning
Extra virgin olive oil for drizzling

Preparation:

1. Switch the air-fryer to 200°C and preheat for 10 minutes. 2. Spray potatoes and cauliflower with oil. Add salt and pepper. 3. Place them in the air-fryer dish and cook for about 15 minutes. Shake them halfway through. 4. Once crisp and golden brown, remove from the air-fryer. 5. In a saucepan, melt butter and cook onions until translucent. Add cooked cauliflowers and potatoes with the stock and milk and cook for 10 minutes. 6. Once the vegetables are soft, blend the soup until smooth. 7. Check the seasoning, and you can add salt and pepper as per your liking. Stir double cream and heat the soup again. 8. Garnish with parsley and drizzle olive oil.

Serving Suggestions: Serve with crusted bread

Variation Tip: You can sprinkle cayenne pepper for variation in taste.

Nutritional Information per Serving: Calories: 317 | Fat: 23g | Sat Fat: 14g | Carbohydrates: 18g | Fiber: 4g | Sugar: 11g | Protein: 8g

Vegan Wellington

⏱ **Prep Time: 30 minutes**   🍽 **Cook: 60 minutes**   🍃 **Serves: 8**

Ingredients:

2 tablespoons olive oil
85g finely chopped sage
510g butternut squash, peeled and cubed
2 shallots, finely chopped
3 garlic cloves, crushed
510g mushrooms, chopped
150ml double cream
½ teaspoon ground mace
200g fresh breadcrumbs
140g cooked chestnuts, chopped
½ teaspoon grated nutmeg for grating
510g block puff pastry
400g cooked beetroot – cubed
1 egg, beaten, to glaze

Preparation:

1. Switch the air fryer to 95°C and preheat for 10 minutes. 2. Spray oil on the cubes of butternut squash, sage, and seasoning. Air fry for 15 minutes until tender. 3. In a large pan, add oil and sauté shallots until translucent. Add mushrooms, garlic, and remaining sage, and fry for 15 minutes. 4. Once all the liquid evaporates, add bread crumbs, mace, nutmeg, cream, chestnuts, roasted squash, beets, and garlic. Once done, let it cool down before assembling the wellington. 5. Roll the pastry and spoon the vegetable mixture along the length of the puff pastry. Fold the pastry and tuck it in from all sides. 6. Brush with egg wash and put it in the fridge for 20 minutes.7. Once chilled, cook in the air fryer for 30 minutes until golden brown and puffed. 8. Dish out and serve warm.

Serving Suggestions: Serve with yoghurt sauce
Variation Tip: You can use vegetables of your choice.
Nutritional Information per Serving: Calories: 543 | Fat: 32g | Sat Fat: 15g | Carbohydrates: 50g | Fiber: 6g | Sugar: 10g | Protein: 11g

Cheesy Vegetable Casserole

⏱ **Prep Time: 20 minutes**   🍽 **Cook: 45 minutes**   🍃 **Serves: 6**

Ingredients:

1 tablespoon olive oil
1 onion, finely chopped
3 garlic cloves, sliced
½ teaspoon ground cumin
1 teaspoon smoked paprika
1 tablespoon dried thyme
2 medium sticks of celery, finely sliced
3 medium carrots, sliced
1 red pepper, chopped
1 yellow pepper, chopped
2 x 400g cans of tomatoes
240ml vegetable stock
140g courgettes, sliced thickly
2 sprigs of fresh thyme
240ml cooked lentils
200g cheddar cheese, grated

Preparation:

1. Heat olive oil in a large pan. Add chopped onions and cook until softened. 2. Add garlic, ground cumin, and smoked paprika, along with carrots, celery, chopped yellow pepper, and chopped red pepper. Let it cook for 5 minutes. 3. Add tomatoes and vegetable stock, along with sliced courgettes and sprigs of fresh thyme. Let it cook for 20 - 25 minutes till all the flavors are released. 4. Finally, add cooked lentils and let it simmer for another 5 minutes. 5. Transfer the cooked veggies to a heat-proof dish and top with grated cheddar cheese and dried thyme. 6. Switch the air fryer to 150°C and preheat for 10 minutes. Cook the casserole in the air fryer for 10 minutes until the cheese has melted 7. Serve hot!

Serving Suggestions: Serve with rice, mash, or quinoa.
Variation Tip: Add any seasonings of your choice for taste variation.
Nutritional Information per Serving: Calories: 216 | Fat: 5.1g | Sat Fat: 0.7g | Carbohydrates: 31g | Fiber: 9.8g | Sugar: 16.1g | Protein: 12.3g

Parmesan Carrot Fries

⏱ Prep Time: 10 minutes   🍲 Cook: 20 minutes   ❧ Serves: 2

Ingredients:

3-4 Carrots
1 tablespoon Olive Oil
1 clove Garlic, crushed
2 tablespoons Grated Parmesan
1 pinch salt and freshly cracked black pepper, optional
1 teaspoon fresh parsley, chopped

Preparation:

1. Add crushed garlic to the olive and stir well. 2. Cut the carrots in the form of fries and toss olive oil and garlic mixture. 3. Mix the parmesan with salt and black pepper. 4. Toss carrots in the parmesan mixture. 5. Add carrot fries on an air fryer basket in an even layer. 6. Air fry at 175°C for 16-20 minutes. Shake halfway through for crispier carrot fries. 7. Top with freshly chopped parsley. 8. Serve warm and enjoy.

Serving Suggestions: Serve with garlic mayo dip.
Variation Tip: You can top it up with crushed red peppers.
Nutritional Information per Serving: Calories: 202 | Fat: 13g | Sat Fat: 5g | Carbohydrates: 13.5g | Fiber: 3g | Sugar: 6g | Protein: 10g

Chili Parsnip and Cauliflower Soup

⏱ Prep Time: 10 minutes   🍲 Cook: 30 minutes   ❧ Serves: 4

Ingredients:

1 tablespoon olive oil
55g butter
310g cauliflower florets
200g parsnips, chopped
960ml vegetable stock
1 tablespoon fennel seed
3 green chilies, deseeded and chopped
2 onions, chopped
3 garlic cloves, sliced
1 teaspoon grated ginger
1 tablespoon lemon juice
½ teaspoon lemon zest
1 tablespoon chives, chopped
Salt and pepper for seasoning

Preparation:

1. Switch the air fryer to 200°C. preheat for 5 minutes. 2. Add parsnips and cauliflower florets to a heat-proof dish. Drizzle oil and season with salt and pepper. Add one cup of vegetable stock to the dish as well. 3. Cook vegetables in the air fryer for 20 minutes until they are soft. 4. In a pan, heat butter and sauté onion along with ginger and garlic. 5. Transfer cooked vegetables to the pan along with fennel seeds, chopped chilies, lemon juice and lemon zest. 6. Add the remaining vegetable stock and bring it to a boil. Once boiled, let it simmer for 10 minutes.7. Blend with the stick blender until it is smooth in consistency. 8. Ladle out in the bowls, sprinkle with chives and serve.

Serving Suggestions: Serve with crusted bread.
Variation Tip: You can drizzle melted butter and chili flakes.
Nutritional Information per Serving: Calories: 133 | Fat: 4g | Sat Fat: 1g | Carbohydrates: 18g | Fiber: 9g | Sugar: 11g | Protein: 7g

Thyme Roasted Vegetables

🕐 **Prep Time: 10 minutes** 🍲 **Cook: 20 minutes** 🍃 **Serves: 4**

Ingredients:

3 tablespoons olive oil
1 aubergine, cut into chunks
2 carrots, cut in lengthwise
2 parsnips, cut in lengthwise
1 red onion, cut into wedges
2 courgettes, cut into chunks
4 garlic cloves smashed
3 sprigs of thyme
200g cherry tomatoes
A handful of basil leaves
Zest of 1 lemon
Lemon Juice 2 tablespoons
Salt and pepper

Preparation:

1. Switch the air fryer to 150°C. Preheat for 10 minutes. 2. Place vegetables in a heat-proof platter that fits in the air fryer. 3. Mix garlic, oil, lemon zest, lemon juice, basil leaves, salt, and pepper in the vegetables. 4. Cook the vegetables in the air fryer for 20 minutes. 5. Serve them as a side dish once cooked and crisped.
Serving Suggestions: You can serve it with hummus
Variation Tip: you can add a variety of your favorite vegetables.
Nutritional Information per Serving: Calories: 198 | Fat: 12g | Sat Fat: 3g |
Carbohydrates: 12g | Fiber: 7g | Sugar: 11g | Protein: 6g

Cheesy Stuffed Peppers

🕐 **Prep Time: 15 minutes** 🍲 **Cook: 20 minutes** 🍃 **Serves: 4**

Ingredients:

2 large peppers, halved, deseeded but stalks left on
200g chopped tomatoes
1 red onion, halved and sliced
1 garlic clove, finely grated
Salt and pepper
1 red chili, deseeded and finely chopped
1 small aubergine cut into small cubes
1 large egg
1 teaspoon pumpkin spice mix
115g low-fat feta cheese, crumbled
140g low-fat fromage frais

Preparation:

1. Switch the air-fryer to 85°C. 2. Place peppers, skin-side up, in the air fryer and roast for 10 minutes. Once done, remove from the air fryer and set aside. 3. For the filling: Add tomatoes, onions, garlic, and aubergine in a pan and cook for 10 minutes. Season with salt and pepper. 4. In a bowl, beat egg, formage frais and feta. 5. In a dish, place peppers and fill with the vegetable mixture generously. 6. Press down from the back of the spoon and fill as much as you can. Top it up with feta mixture and sprinkle pumpkin spice. 7. Cook stuffed peppers in the air fryer for 10 minutes until the topping is firm. 8. Serve warm.
Serving Suggestions: Serve with a green salad and lime wedges
Variation Tip: Add in some cayenne pepper for taste enhancement.
Nutritional Information per Serving: Calories: 288 | Fat: 7g | Sat Fat: 3g |
Carbohydrates: 39g | Fiber: 15g | Sugar: 26g | Protein: 19g

Cheesy Tuna-Stuffed Potatoes

⏰ Prep Time: 30 minutes 🍲 Cook: 45 minutes 🌿 Serves: 2

Ingredients:

2 potatoes (about 450g)
½ tablespoon sunflower oil
A pinch of salt and black pepper, to taste
For Toppings:
115g cheddar cheese,
115g shredded tuna
3 tablespoons mayonnaise
Parsley for garnishing

Preparation:

1. Switch the air-fryer to 200°C and preheat for 10 minutes. 2. Wash potatoes thoroughly and dry them with a tea towel. 3. Rub oil on the potato›s skin and sprinkle salt and pepper. 4. Line potatoes in the air fryer and cook for 40 minutes until they are tender. Check by inserting a skewer or fork. 5. Change the side after 20 minutes. 6. Once cooked, the skin should be crispy. 7. Cut potatoes in half, lengthwise. 8. Scoop out some of the potato flesh and set aside. 9. Prepare filling: In a bowl, add mayonnaise and shredded tuna. 10. Fill potato halves with the filling and add chopped parsley and shredded cheese on top. 11. Put these back in the air fryer for 5 minutes until the cheese is melted. 12. Dish out and serve warm.
Serving Suggestions: You can serve it as a side dish with steak.
Variation Tip: You can also add the sausage meat, bacon or ham to the filling.
Nutritional Information per Serving: Calories: 206 | Fat: 2g | Sat Fat: 0.4g | Carbohydrates: 40g | Fiber: 5g | Sugar: 3g | Protein: 5g

Roasted Broccoli and Stilton Soup

⏰ Prep Time: 10 minutes 🍲 Cook: 15 minutes 🌿 Serves: 4

Ingredients:

2 tablespoons rapeseed oil
1 onion, finely chopped
1 stick celery, sliced
Salt and pepper for seasoning
1 leek, sliced
1 medium potato, diced
2 tablespoons of butter
960ml vegetable stock
450g broccoli, roughly chopped
140g stilton, or other blue cheese, crumbled

Preparation:

1. Switch the air fryer to 40°C and preheat for 5 minutes. 2. Spray broccoli with oil and cook in the air fryer for 5 minutes. 3. In a pan, add butter and sauté onion till translucent. Add celery, leeks, and potatoes along with the vegetable stock. Bring it to a boil and simmer till the potatoes are soft. 4. Then add broccoli and let it simmer for 10 minutes. 5. Blend with the stick blender and add crumbled stilton. Season with salt and pepper. 6. Ladle out in bowls and Serve warm.
Serving Suggestions: You can garnish with croutons.
Variation Tip: You can use any other crumbled blue cheese.
Nutritional Information per Serving: Calories: 340 | Fat: 21g | Sat Fat: 9.6g | Carbohydrates: 13.8 | Fiber: 6.9g | Sugar: 5g | Protein: 24.3g

Cream Carrot Soup with Pancetta Bread

⏱ **Prep Time: 15 minutes**   🍲 **Cook: 45 minutes**   ❦ **Serves: 2**

Ingredients:

710g carrot, cut into cubes
720ml vegetable stock
4 garlic cloves with skin
A few thyme sprigs, plus an extra to garnish
2 tablespoons of butter
2 onions, finely chopped
6 tablespoons double cream
2 tablespoons olive oil
Salt and pepper
6 slices pancetta
2 thick slices of rustic bread

Preparation:

1. Switch the air-fryer to 200°C and preheat for 10 minutes. 2. Toss carrots with oil, garlic, and rosemary sprigs and air fry for 20 minutes. 3. In a saucepan, heat butter and sauté onions. Dump in the roasted carrots, discard sprigs of thyme, and pour vegetable stock. 4. Let it simmer for 20 minutes and season with salt and pepper. 5. Blend it with a stick blender to get a smooth consistency. 6. Add 5 tablespoons of cream and mix well. Adjust seasoning as needed. 7. Air fry pancetta and bread slices at 95°C for 5 minutes until crisp. 8. Ladle out soup in the serving bowl and garnish cream over it. 9. Serve with bread and crisped pancetta.

Serving Suggestions: Serve topped with cilantro.
Variation Tip: You can also use chicken or beef stock instead of vegetable stock.
Nutritional Information per Serving: Calories: 828 | Fat: 57g | Sat Fat: 26g | Carbohydrates: 51g | Fiber: 12g | Sugar: 34g | Protein: 28g

Rosemary Potato Soup

⏱ **Prep Time: 10 minutes**   🍲 **Cook: 40 minutes**   ❦ **Serves: 2**

Ingredients:

200g chopped vegetables such as onions, celery, and carrots
480ml potatoes, cubed
2 tablespoons butter
1 onion chopped
1 sprig of rosemary
1 tablespoon oil
2 cloves of garlic, smashed
960ml chicken stock
Salt and pepper
2 tablespoons crème fraîche
1 teaspoon chopped parsley to serve

Preparation:

1. Switch the air-fryer to 200°C and preheat for 10 minutes. 2. Drizzle oil on the vegetables and coat well. Place vegetables in the dish and air fry them for about 20 minutes. 3. Remove the vegetable once they are soft. 4. In a saucepan, add butter and sauté onions until translucent. Add garlic, roasted vegetables, and rosemary along with the stock. 5. Let it simmer for 20 minutes. Once the flavors are mingled well, discard the rosemary sprig and blend everything with the stick blender. 6. You should get a smooth consistency. Check the seasoning and add according to your liking. 7. Ladle out in the soup bowls and garnish with crème fraîche and chopped parsley.

Serving Suggestions: Serve with crusted bread
Variation Tip: You can add crumbled blue cheese as well.
Nutritional Information per Serving: Calories: 218 | Fat: 7g | Sat Fat: 6g | Carbohydrates: 32g | Fiber: 6g | Sugar: 7g | Protein: 4g

Cream and Cheese Stuffed Pumpkin

⏱ **Prep Time: 10 minutes** 🍲 **Cook: 40 minutes** 🍃 **Serves: 6**

Ingredients:

450g pumpkin (that can fit in the air fryer basket)
160ml milk
300ml double cream
3 garlic cloves, crushed
85g grated parmesan
2 teaspoons thyme leaves
A pinch of black pepper

Preparation:

1. Switch the air fryer to 175°C and preheat for 10 minutes. 2. Wash the pumpkin and slice off the head. Scoop out the strands and seeds. 3. Place the pumpkin in the air fryer tray. 4. In a saucepan, heat milk, cream, thyme, and garlic till they start bubbling. 5. Pour the cream mixture into the pumpkin and add half of the parmesan. 6. Put the head back on the pumpkin. 7. Air fry pumpkin for 30 minutes. 8. Sprinkle black pepper and remaining parmesan cheese and air fry for another 10 minutes until the cheese turns golden. 9. Serve with toasted bread slices.

Serving Suggestions: Garnish with basil leaves, parsley, and chili flakes.
Variation Tip: You can also garnish it with roasted pancetta for taste variation.
Nutritional Information per Serving: Calories: 342 | Fat: 32g | Sat Fat: 18g | Carbohydrates: 6g | Fiber: 2g | Sugar: 5g | Protein: 8g

Cheese Vegetable Pie

⏱ **Prep Time: 15 minutes** 🍲 **Cook: 40 minutes** 🍃 **Serves: 4**

Ingredients:

4 tablespoons butter
310g ready-to-cook, short crust pastry
600ml milk
Salt and pepper
90g broccoli florets
150g frozen peas
2 teaspoons mustard powder
85g grated cheddar cheese
2 large potatoes, cut into small chunks
100g cauliflower florets
30g flour
1 egg lightly beaten

Preparation:

1. Prepare sauce: Melt butter and stir mustard and flour. Add milk gradually. Cook it until the sauce is thick and creamy. Fold in cheese until it is melted. 2. Switch the air fryer to 150°C and preheat for 10 minutes. 3. In a large pan, boil potatoes, broccoli, peas, and cauliflower one by one. Drain and pat dry. 4. Dump boiled vegetables in a mixing bowl and add creamy sauce. Fold the sauce carefully. Season with salt and pepper. 5. Roll pie crust until ¼inches thick. 6. Add vegetables to a deep dish and cover it with the pie crust. Make 3-4 slits on the crust and brush with the egg. 7. Place the pie dish in the air fryer and cook for 40 minutes until it is golden brown. 8. Serve and enjoy.

Serving Suggestions: Sprinkle some seasoning over the pie and serve.
Variation Tip: You can use a variety of other vegetables for the dish.
Nutritional Information per Serving: Calories: 604 | Fat: 34g | Sat Fat: 19g | Carbohydrates: 45g | Fiber: 9g | Sugar: 14g | Protein: 33g

Chapter 4 Fish and Seafood Recipes

Crispy Fish and Chips

⏱ **Prep Time: 5 minutes**   🍲 **Cook: 18 minutes**   🍽 **Serves: 4**

> **Ingredients:**

455g cod fillet cut into strips
65g flour
½ teaspoon garlic powder
2 teaspoons paprika
½ teaspoon salt
¼ teaspoon black pepper
50g bread crumbs
1 large egg
Cooking oil spray
115g frozen chips

> **Preparation:**

1. Preheat air fryer at 200°C for 10 minutes. 2. In a bowl add flour and season it with salt, pepper, garlic powder and paprika. 3. In another bowl beat the egg and set aside. 4. Take out bread crumbs in a relatively deep platter and set aside. 5. Pat dry fish fillets and coat them with flash then dunk them in the egg and lastly roll them in bread crumbs. 6. Spray oil on both sides of the fillets. 7. Place the fish fillets in the air fry basket in a single layer and cook them for 10 minutes, flipping them halfway through the cook time. 8. Next reduce the air fry temperature to 180°C and place the chips in the air fryer basket. Cook for 8 minutes and toss them halfway through the cook time. 9. Serve
Serving Suggestions: Serve with tartar sauce and lemon wedges.
Variation Tip: You can also serve with marinara sauce for variation in flavor.
Nutritional Information per Serving: Calories: 200 | Fat: 2g | Sat Fat: 1g | Carbohydrates: 18g | Fiber: 1g | Sugar: 1g | Protein: 24g

Easy Crab Cakes

⏱ **Prep Time: 5 minutes**   🍲 **Cook: 10 minutes**   🍽 **Serves: 4**

> **Ingredients:**

250g crabs, finely chopped
Cooking spray
75g whole-wheat panko breadcrumbs
2 tablespoons Thai sweet chili sauce
1 large egg
¼ teaspoon ground pepper
3 tablespoons fresh coriander, finely chopped
2 tablespoons mayonnaise
⅛ teaspoon salt
2 lime wedges

> **Preparation:**

1. Switch the temperature of the Air fryer to 200°C. 2. In a bowl, merge crab meat, panko, coriander, chili sauce, mayonnaise, egg, salt, and black pepper. 3. Mix well and form cakes 8cm in diameter. 4. Position the cakes inside the Air fryer basket and spray with cooking spray. 5. Air fry for about 10 minutes, flipping once in between. 6. Dish out and serve garnished with lemon wedges.
Serving Suggestions: Serve with tomato ketchup.
Variation Tip: You can use fish instead of crabs.
Nutritional Information per Serving: Calories: 399 | Fat: 15.5g | Sat Fat: 2.1g | Carbohydrates: 27.9g | Fiber: 2.8g | Sugar: 9.8g | Protein: 34.6g

Breaded Scallops with Remoulade Sauce

⏱ Prep Time: 20 minutes 🍲 Cook: 6 minutes 🍃 Serves: 4

Ingredients:

For the Scallops:
60g seasoned panko breadcrumbs
2 tablespoons butter, melted
Kosher salt
1 egg, beaten
1 teaspoon Old Bay seasoning
450g sea scallops
120g all-purpose flour
1 lemon, cut into wedges for serving
For the Remoulade Sauce:
1 tablespoon Dijon mustard
240ml mayonnaise
1 tablespoon lemon juice
1 tablespoon parsley, chopped
1 clove garlic, minced
1 tablespoon Louisiana-style hot sauce
1 scallion, thinly sliced
1 teaspoon Cajun seasoning

Preparation:

1. Switch the temperature of the Air fryer to 200°C. 2. In a small bowl, merge the bread crumbs, melted butter, and Old Bay. 3. Dust the scallops with salt. 4. In a shallow bowl, spread flour, and in a third bowl, whip egg. 5. Dip the scallops in the egg mixture after dredging them in the flour mixture. 6. Coat with the panko and layer the scallops into the Air fryer basket. 7. Cook for 6 minutes, flipping once in between. 8. For the remoulade sauce: Merge all the ingredients for Remoulade sauce. 9. Dish out the scallops and serve with the sauce.
Serving Suggestions: Serve topped with lemon wedges.
Variation Tip: You can add chili flakes too.
Nutritional Information per Serving: Calories: 630 | Fat: 31.4g | Sat Fat: 7.1g | Carbohydrates: 59.9g | Fiber: 2.5g | Sugar: 4.5g | Protein: 27.8g

Halibut with Yuca Fries

⏱ Prep Time: 5 minutes 🍲 Cook: 20 minutes 🍃 Serves: 8

Ingredients:

455g. yuca, peeled and cut into sticks
2 teaspoons paprika
65g flour
½ teaspoon garlic powder
¼ teaspoon black pepper
55g panko bread crumbs
Cooking oil spray
½ teaspoon salt
1 large egg beaten
455g. halibut fillets, cut into strips

Preparation:

1. Switch the temperature of the Air fryer to 200°C. 2. In a small bowl, merge flour with garlic powder, paprika, salt, and black pepper. 3. Now, put the bread crumbs in a bowl, and whisk egg in another bowl. 4. Dredge the fish into the flour mixture, and then dip into the egg mixture. 5. Finally, coat evenly with the breadcrumbs and spray lightly with oil. 6. Layer the fish in the air fryer basket and cook for 12 minutes, flipping halfway. 7. Dish out the fish and add yuca fries to the Air fryer basket. 8. Air fry for about 8 minutes and dish out to serve with the fish.
Serving Suggestions: You can serve with tartar sauce.
Variation Tip: You can use haddock or cod instead of halibut.
Nutritional Information per Serving: Calories: 200 | Fat: 18g | Sat Fat: 1g | Carbohydrates: 18g | Fiber: 1g | Sugar: 1g | Protein: 24g

Air Fryer Herbed Salmon

⏰ **Prep Time: 5 minutes**   🍳 **Cook: 10 minutes**   📚 **Serves: 4**

Ingredients:

1 teaspoon salt
1 teaspoon mixed herbs
4 salmon fillets
1 teaspoon black pepper
1 teaspoon garlic granules
½ tablespoon olive oil

Preparation:

1. Switch the temperature of the Air fryer to 180°C. 2. In a bowl, merge the salt, mixed herbs, black pepper, and garlic granules. 3. Rub a little olive oil over each salmon fillet and then coat gently with the seasoning. 4. Layer salmon fillets in the Air fryer basket and then air fry for about 10 minutes. 5. Dish out and serve warm.
Serving Suggestions: Serve with cooked seasonal greens and quinoa.
Variation Tip: You can also use cod instead of salmon.
Nutritional Information per Serving: Calories: 253 | Fat: 12.8g | Sat Fat: 1.8g | Carbohydrates: 0.7g | Fiber: 0.2g | Sugar: 0g | Protein: 34.7g

Garlicky Cod Loins

⏰ **Prep Time: 10 minutes**   🍳 **Cook: 10 minutes**   📚 **Serves: 4**

Ingredients:

4 tablespoons butter, melted
4 cod loins
6 garlic cloves, minced
2 tablespoons fresh dill, chopped
2 tablespoons lemon juice
½ teaspoon salt

Preparation:

1. Switch the temperature of the Air fryer to 185°C. 2. In a small bowl, merge the cod fillets with butter, garlic, lemon juice, dill, and salt. 3. Layer the cod in the Air fryer basket and then air fry for 10 minutes. 4. Dish out the cod and serve warm.
Serving Suggestions: Serve with baked asparagus.
Variation Tip: You can also use more herbs.
Nutritional Information per Serving: Calories: 204 | Fat: 12.7g | Sat Fat: 7.5g | Carbohydrates: 2.5g | Fiber: 0.3g | Sugar: 0.2g | Protein: 20.8g

Crispy Tilapia Fillets

⏰ **Prep Time: 5 minutes**   🍳 **Cook: 12 minutes**   📚 **Serves: 2**

Ingredients:

30g flour
1 tablespoon cornstarch
2 tilapia fillets
1 egg
¼ teaspoon salt and pepper
1 teaspoon paprika
3 tablespoons Old Bay seasoning
1 tablespoon water
Cooking spray

Preparation:

1. Switch the temperature of the Air fryer to 200°C. 2. In a small bowl, merge all the seasonings. 3. In a bowl, whisk eggs with water and in another bowl, spread flour. 4. Dip the tilapia in the egg mixture after dredging them in the flour mixture. 5. Coat with the seasonings mixture and layer the tilapia into the Air fryer basket. 6. Cook for 12 minutes, flipping once in between. 7. Dish out and serve warm.
Serving Suggestions: You can serve with tartar sauce or ketchup.
Variation Tip: You can also use butter instead of oil.
Nutritional Information per Serving: Calories: 149 | Fat: 5g | Sat Fat: 1g | Carbohydrates: 16g | Fiber: 1g | Sugar: 2.2g | Protein: 10g

Crispy Anchovies with Lemon

⏱ Prep Time: 10 minutes 🍲 Cook: 6 minutes 🌿 Serves: 4

Ingredients:

120g all-purpose flour
450g blue anchovies
1 tablespoon kosher salt

1 lemon, cut into wedges
1 tablespoon peanut oil

Preparation:

1. Switch the temperature of the Air fryer to 175°C. 2. In a small bowl, merge the flour and salt. 3. Dredge the anchovies in the flour mixture. 4. Layer the anchovies into the Air fryer basket. 5. Cook for 6 minutes, flipping once in between. 6. Dish out and serve warm with lemon wedges.

Serving Suggestions: Serve with basil on top.

Variation Tip: Add red chili flakes to spice up the taste.

Nutritional Information per Serving: Calories: 493 | Fat: 24g | Sat Fat: 5g | Carbohydrates: 46g | Fiber: 6g | Sugar: 8g | Protein: 28g

Honey Glazed Salmon

⏱ Prep Time: 10 minutes 🍲 Cook: 9 minutes 🌿 Serves: 4

Ingredients:

2 tablespoons soy sauce
4 salmon fillets, boneless
3 tablespoons honey

1 teaspoon sesame seeds
1 teaspoon sea salt

Preparation:

1. Switch the temperature of the Air fryer to 190°C. 2. In a small bowl, merge the soy sauce, honey and sea salt. 3. Rub the salmon with half of the glaze. 4. Layer the salmon in the Air fryer basket and then air fry for 7 minutes. 5. Dish out and trickle with the remaining glaze and sesame seeds. 6. Air fry again for 2 minutes and serve.

Serving Suggestions: Serve with baked asparagus.

Variation Tip: Add 1 teaspoon of chili flakes to the honey glaze for increased spiciness.

Nutritional Information per Serving: Calories: 292 | Fat: 11.4g | Sat Fat: 1.6g | Carbohydrates: 13.8g | Fiber: 0.2g | Sugar: 13.1g | Protein: 35.2g

Baked Lemony Rainbow Trout

⏱ Prep Time: 5 minutes 🍲 Cook: 12 minutes 🌿 Serves: 4

Ingredients:

3 tablespoons olive oil
4 (115g) Rainbow trout fillets
2 teaspoons lemon juice
2 teaspoons fresh parsley
½ teaspoon paprika

¼ teaspoon black pepper
2 cloves garlic, minced
2 teaspoons fresh dill
¾ teaspoon sea salt
Thin lemon slices

Preparation:

1. Switch the temperature of the Air fryer to 200°C. 2. In a small bowl, merge the trout with olive oil, garlic, lemon juice, dill, parsley, and paprika. 3. Dust both sides of trout with sea salt and black pepper. 4. Layer the trout into the Air fryer basket and top with thin lemon slices. 5. Cook for 12 minutes and dish out to serve warm.

Serving Suggestions: Serve with balsamic onions.

Variation Tip: You can use any fresh herbs of your choice.

Nutritional Information per Serving: Calories: 271 | Fat: 21.4g | Sat Fat: 4.2g | Carbohydrates: 5.1g | Fiber: 0.3g | Sugar: 1.5g | Protein: 17.8g

Air Fryer Lemon Mackerel Fillets

⏱ Prep Time: 3 minutes 🍲 Cook: 10 minutes 🍃 Serves: 2

Ingredients:

⅓ teaspoons salt
2 mackerel fillets
Black pepper, to taste
1 pinch cumin
½ lemon
½ teaspoon garlic powder

Preparation:

1. Switch the temperature of the Air fryer to 200°C. 2. In a small bowl, dust the mackerel fillets with salt, pepper, cumin, and garlic powder. 3. Layer the mackerel fillets over lemon slices into the Air fryer basket and then air fry for 10 minutes, flipping once in between. 4. Dish out and serve warm.
Serving Suggestions: Serve with pickled onions.
Variation Tip: You can use any fish of your choice.
Nutritional Information per Serving: Calories: 242 | Fat: 16g | Sat Fat: 4g | Carbohydrates: 3g | Fiber: 1g | Sugar: 1g | Protein: 21g

Crispy Spicy Oysters

⏱ Prep Time: 15 minutes 🍲 Cook: 12 minutes 🍃 Serves: 4

Ingredients:

60g flour
2 cans oysters, 225g each
1 teaspoon Cajun seasoning
½ teaspoon black pepper

3 tablespoons hot sauce
1 teaspoon salt
2 eggs
120g Panko bread crumbs

Preparation:

1. Switch the temperature of the Air fryer to 175°C. 2. In a small bowl, place panko. 3. In another bowl, whisk egg with hot sauce and in a third bowl, merge flour, Cajun seasoning, salt, and pepper. 4. Dip the oysters in the egg mixture after dredging them in the flour mixture. 5. Coat with the panko and layer the oysters into the Air fryer basket. 6. Cook for 12 minutes, flipping once in between. 7. Dish out and serve warm.
Serving Suggestions: You can serve it with coleslaw.
Variation Tip: You can also use Old Bay seasoning.
Nutritional Information per Serving: Calories: 337 | Fat: 6.3g | Sat Fat: 1.6g | Carbohydrates: 54.2g | Fiber: 3.4g | Sugar: 4.4g | Protein: 15.1g

Air Fryer Pickled Halibut with Onion

⏱ Prep Time: 10 minutes 🍲 Cook: 20 minutes 🍃 Serves: 2

Ingredients:

½ white onion, thinly sliced
2 pieces halibut
1 lemon, thinly sliced
115g butter
120nl pickle juice
Real dill herb
120ml salsa

Preparation:

1. Switch the temperature of the Air fryer to 175°C. 2. In the Air fryer tray, layer onions and butter, followed by lemon and halibut. 3. Top with pickle juice and cook for about 10 minutes. 4. Now, add salsa and dill herb, and cook for 10 more minutes. 5. Dish out and serve warm.
Serving Suggestions: Serve garnished with cilantro.
Variation Tip: You can use your favorite salsa.
Nutritional Information per Serving: Calories: 829 | Fat: 60g | Sat Fat: 30.1g | Carbohydrates: 10.7g | Fiber: 2.6g | Sugar: 4.4g | Protein: 62.7g

Crispy Cod

⏰ **Prep Time:** 10 minutes   🍲 **Cook:** 12 minutes   🍃 **Serves:** 4

Ingredients:

40g polenta
1 pound cod, about 1-inch thick, cut into 4 pieces
30g plain flour
1½ teaspoons garlic salt
½ teaspoon ground black pepper
Olive oil cooking spray
1½ teaspoons seafood seasoning
1 teaspoon onion powder
½ teaspoon paprika

Preparation:

1. Switch the temperature of the Air fryer to 195°C. 2. In a small bowl, merge the cod fillets with flour, polenta, seafood seasoning, onion powder, garlic salt, pepper, and paprika. 3. Spray the sides of cod with cooking spray. Layer the cod into the Air fryer basket and then air fry for 12 minutes, flipping once in between. 4. Dish out the cod and serve warm.
Serving Suggestions: Serve with sweet and sour coleslaw.
Variation Tip: You can use Old Bay seasoning.
Nutritional Information per Serving: Calories: 171 | Fat: 2g | Sat Fat: 0g | Carbohydrates: 15g | Fiber: 1g | Sugar: 1g | Protein: 23g

Fried Oysters with Cheesy Garlic Butter

⏰ **Prep Time:** 10 minutes   🍲 **Cook:** 7 minutes   🍃 **Serves:** 4

Ingredients:

½ stick butter, melted
8 oysters on the half shell
2 tablespoons lemon juice
2 garlic cloves, grated
1 teaspoon Worcestershire sauce
25g Parmigiano Reggiano, grated
1 tablespoon fresh parsley, chopped
Salt, cayenne, and black pepper, to taste

Preparation:

1. Switch the temperature of the Air fryer to 175°C. 2. In a large bowl, merge butter, garlic, Worcestershire sauce, parsley, lemon juice, cheese, salt, cayenne, and pepper. 3. Layer oysters in the Air fryer basket and then cook for about 2 minutes. 4. Dish out and top each oyster with 1 tablespoon of the butter mixture. 5. Top with cheese and cook for about 5 minutes. 6. Serve hot.
Serving Suggestions: Serve with cocktail sauce or your favorite dipping sauce.
Variation Tip: Serve with bread and hot sauce.
Nutritional Information per Serving: Calories: 215 | Fat: 16.1g | Sat Fat: 9.3g | Carbohydrates: 5.5g | Fiber: 0.1g | Sugar: 1.5g | Protein: 11.8g

White Fish Fillets with Pesto Sauce

⏰ **Prep Time:** 10 minutes   🍲 **Cook:** 8 minutes   🍃 **Serves:** 3

Ingredients:

1 tablespoon olive oil
3 white fish fillets
Salt and black pepper, to taste
2 garlic cloves
1 tablespoon parmesan cheese, grated
1 bunch fresh basil
2 tablespoons pine nuts
240ml olive oil, extra-virgin

Preparation:

1. Switch the temperature of the Air fryer to 180°C. 2. Dust the fish fillets evenly with salt and pepper, and rub olive oil over it. 3. Layer the fish fillets into the Air fryer basket and then air fry for 8 minutes, flipping once in between. 4. Meanwhile, in a food processor, blitz garlic, basil leaves, pine nuts, parmesan cheese and olive oil. 5. Dish out and serve drizzled with pesto sauce.
Serving Suggestions: Serve with ketchup if desired.
Variation Tip: You can also serve with cream cheese.
Nutritional Information per Serving: Calories: 890 | Fat: 83.2g | Sat Fat: 12g | Carbohydrates: 1.6g | Fiber: 0.3g | Sugar: 0.2g | Protein: 39.4g

Trout with Steamed Vegetables

⏰ **Prep Time:** 10 minutes 🍲 **Cook:** 21 minutes 🔖 **Serves:** 2

Ingredients:

1 trout
1 teaspoon salt
60g cauliflower
45g broccoli

Preparation:

1. Switch the temperature of the Air fryer to 200°C. 2. Steam cook the vegetables for about 6 minutes. 3. Dust the trout with salt. 4. Layer the trout into the Air fryer basket and then air fry for 15 minutes, flipping once in between. 5. Dish out the trout and serve warm with steamed veggies.
Serving Suggestions: Serve topped with lemon wedges.
Variation Tip: You can also steam some other vegetables.
Nutritional Information per Serving: Calories: 132 | Fat: 5.4g | Sat Fat: 0.9g | Carbohydrates: 2.8g | Fiber: 1.2g | Sugar: 1g | Protein: 17.7g

Bacon-Wrapped Oyster

⏰ **Prep Time:** 10 minutes 🍲 **Cook:** 13 minutes 🔖 **Serves:** 8

Ingredients:

16 slices bacon, thin-cut
32 small oysters, shucked
Lime or lemon wedges, for serving

Preparation:

1. Switch the temperature of the Air fryer to 175°C. 2. Air fry the bacon for 5 minutes, until they are cooked but not crispy. 3. Wrap half piece of bacon around the oyster and fasten with a toothpick. 4. Cook in the Air fryer for about 8 minutes, turning once in between. 5. Trickle with lemon or lime juice and serve warm.
Serving Suggestions: You can serve topped with lime or lemon wedges.
Variation Tip: You can use scallops instead of oyster too.
Nutritional Information per Serving: Calories: 551 | Fat: 25g | Sat Fat: 8g | Carbohydrates: 24g | Fiber: 1g | Sugar: 1g | Protein: 54g

Marinated Lime Salmon

⏰ **Prep Time:** 10 minutes 🍲 **Cook:** 20 minutes 🔖 **Serves:** 4

Ingredients:

3 tablespoons pure maple syrup
1 lime, zested and juiced
3 tablespoons soy sauce
4 (115g) salmon fillets, skin-on

Preparation:

1. Switch the temperature of the Air fryer to 200°C. 2. In a small bowl, merge the salmon fillets with lime zest and juice, maple syrup, and soy sauce. Marinate for about 2 hours. 3. Layer the salmon, skin side up in Air fryer basket and then air fry for 10 minutes. 4. In a saucepan, simmer leftover marinade for 10 minutes. 5. Dish out the salmon and serve warm with marinade.
Serving Suggestions: Serve over cooked greens.
Variation Tip: You can use coconut aminos instead of soy sauce.
Nutritional Information per Serving: Calories: 201 | Fat: 7.1g | Sat Fat: 1g | Carbohydrates: 12.7g | Fiber: 0.6g | Sugar: 9.4g | Protein: 22.9g

Chapter 5 Poultry Recipes

Southern Fried Chicken

⏰ **Prep Time: 15 minutes**   **Cook time: 26 minutes**   **Serves: 4**

Ingredients:

120ml buttermilk
2 teaspoons salt, plus 1 tablespoon
1 teaspoon freshly ground black pepper
455g chicken thighs and drumsticks

120g plain flour
2 teaspoons onion powder
2 teaspoons garlic powder
½ teaspoon sweet paprika

Preparation:

1. In a large mixing bowl, whisk together the buttermilk, 2 teaspoons of salt, and pepper. 2. Add the chicken pieces to the bowl, and let the chicken marinate for at least an hour, covered, in the refrigerator. 3. About 5 minutes before the chicken is done marinating, prepare the dredging mixture. In a large mixing bowl, combine the flour, 1 tablespoon of salt, onion powder, garlic powder, and paprika. 4. Spray the air fryer basket with olive oil. 5. Remove the chicken from the buttermilk mixture and dredge it in the flour mixture. Shake off any excess flour. 6. Place the chicken pieces into the greased air fryer basket in a single layer, leaving space between each piece. Spray the chicken generously with olive oil. 7. Air-fry the chicken pieces at 200°C for 13 minutes, flipping them and spraying them with olive oil halfway through. 8. Reset the timer and fry for 13 minutes more. 9. Check that the chicken has reached an internal temperature of 75°C. Add cooking time if needed. 10. Enjoy!

Serving Suggestions: Pair with coleslaw, mashed potatoes, or a simple green salad for a classic Southern-style meal.

Variation Tip: For extra flavor, add a pinch of cayenne pepper or hot sauce to the buttermilk marinade. Substitute chicken breasts or wings for a different cut.

Nutritional Information per Serving: Calories: 388 | Fat: 19.49g | Sat Fat: 5.3g | Carbohydrates: 28.2g | Fiber: 1.4g | Sugar: 1.7g | Protein: 23.46g

Turkey Meatloaf with Veggie Medley

⏰ **Prep Time: 15 minutes**   **Cook time: 50 minutes**   **Serves: 4**

Ingredients:

For the Meatloaf:
1 large egg
60g ketchup
2 teaspoons Worcestershire sauce
50g Italian-style bread crumbs

1 teaspoon salt
455g turkey mince (93 percent lean)
1 tablespoon vegetable oil

For the Veggie Medley:
2 carrots, thinly sliced
200g green beans, trimmed
180g broccoli florets
1 red pepper, sliced into strips

2 tablespoons vegetable oil
½ teaspoon salt
½ teaspoon freshly ground black pepper

Preparation:

1. In a large bowl, whisk the egg. Stir in the ketchup, Worcestershire sauce, bread crumbs, and salt. Let sit for 5 minutes to allow the bread crumbs to absorb some moisture. 2. Gently mix in the turkey until just incorporated. Form the mixture into a loaf. Brush with the oil. 3. In a large bowl, combine the carrots, green beans, broccoli, pepper, oil, salt, and black pepper. Mix well to coat the vegetables with the oil. 4. Place the meatloaf in the air fryer basket and roast at 175°C for 30 minutes. 5. When cooked, take out the meat; add the vegetables to the basket, and air-fry the food at 200°C for 20 minutes. 6. Serve warm.

Serving Suggestions: Serve with mashed sweet potatoes or a side of quinoa for a complete, balanced meal.

Variation Tip: Add diced onions and garlic to the meatloaf mixture for extra flavor, or swap the veggie medley for zucchini and asparagus.

Nutritional Information per Serving: Calories: 702 | Fat: 62.32g | Sat Fat: 13.2g | Carbohydrates: 11.33g | Fiber: 2.1g | Sugar: 4.94g | Protein: 24.32g

Spicy Chicken Sandwiches

🕐 **Prep Time:** 15 minutes   **Cook time:** 35 minutes   **Serves:** 4

Ingredients:

For the Chicken Sandwiches:
2 tablespoons flour
2 large eggs
2 teaspoons Louisiana-style hot sauce
105g panko bread crumbs
1 teaspoon paprika
½ teaspoon garlic powder
¼ teaspoon salt
¼ teaspoon freshly ground black pepper

¼ teaspoon cayenne pepper (optional)
4 thin-sliced chicken cutlets (100g each)
2 teaspoons vegetable oil
4 hamburger rolls

For the Pickles:
155g dill pickle chips, drained
1 large egg
55g panko bread crumbs

Nonstick cooking spray
120ml ranch dressing, for serving (optional)

Preparation:

1. Set up a breading station with three small shallow bowls. Place the flour in the first bowl. In the second bowl, whisk together the eggs and hot sauce. Combine the panko, paprika, garlic powder, salt, black pepper, and cayenne pepper (if using) in the third bowl. 2. Bread the chicken cutlets in this order: First, dip them into the flour, coating both sides. Then, dip into the egg mixture. Finally, coat them in the panko mixture, gently pressing the breading into the chicken to help it adhere. Drizzle the cutlets with the oil. 3. Pat the pickles dry with a paper towel. 4. In a small shallow bowl, whisk the egg. Add the panko to a second shallow bowl. 5. Dip the pickles in the egg, then the panko. Mist both sides of the pickles with cooking spray. 6. Place the chicken in the air fryer basket and air-fry at 200°C for 18 minutes, flipping halfway through. 7. When cooked, take out the chicken, add the pickles to the basket, and air-fry the food at 205°C for 15 minutes, shaking the basket halfway through cooking. 8. Place one chicken cutlet on each hamburger roll. Serve the "fried" pickles on the side with ranch dressing, if desired.

Serving Suggestions: Serve with a side of sweet potato fries or a fresh coleslaw to complement the heat of the sandwich.

Variation Tip: Swap the ranch dressing for spicy mayo or chipotle aioli for an extra kick.

Nutritional Information per Serving: Calories: 362 | Fat: 11.02g | Sat Fat: 2.5g | Carbohydrates: 32.71g | Fiber: 2g | Sugar: 4.07g | Protein: 31.17g

Chicken Wings with Blue Cheese Dressing

🕐 **Prep Time:** 10 minutes   🍲 **Cook:** 20 minutes   🍽 **Serves:** 4

Ingredients:

900g chicken wings
Nonstick cooking spray
Salt and black pepper, to taste
Blue Cheese Dressing (For Serving):
120ml hot sauce
1 teaspoon Worcestershire sauce
4 tablespoons butter, melted
½ teaspoon garlic powder
30g blue cheese, crumbled

Preparation:

1. Switch the temperature of the Air fryer to 195°C. 2. Dust the wings with salt and black pepper. 3. Grease the air fryer basket with cooking spray. Layer the wings in the Air fryer basket and then air fry for about 20 minutes, flipping once in between. 4. Meanwhile, in a large bowl, merge hot sauce, butter, Worcestershire sauce, blue cheese and garlic powder to make blue cheese dressing. 5. Add wings to the sauce and mix thoroughly. 6. Serve hot.

Serving Suggestions: You can serve it with tartar sauce.

Variation Tip: Add some red chili powder for extra spice.

Nutritional Information per Serving: Calories: 577 | Fat: 32.5g | Sat Fat: 12.7g | Carbohydrates: 1.6g | Fiber: 0.1g | Sugar: 0.9g | Protein: 66.3g

Spicy Chicken Wings

⏰ **Prep Time:** 5 minutes 🍲 **Cook:** 20 minutes 🔖 **Serves:** 4

Ingredients:

900g chicken wings

Seasoning:
½ teaspoon black pepper
1 teaspoon paprika
½ teaspoon onion powder

Sauce:
1 tablespoon butter
180ml hot sauce

1 tablespoon olive oil

¼ teaspoon baking powder
½ teaspoon garlic powder
Salt, to taste

1 teaspoon chili flakes
½ teaspoon garlic powder

Preparation:

1. Switch the temperature of the Air fryer to 195°C. 2. Dust the wings with oil and seasoning mix and marinate for 2 hours. 3. Layer the wings in the Air fryer basket and then air fry for about 20 minutes, flipping once in between. 4. Meanwhile, in a large bowl, merge all the sauce ingredients and cook for 10 minutes in a pan on low heat. 5. Add wings to the sauce and mix thoroughly. 6. Serve hot.
Serving Suggestions: Serve garnished with spring onions and coriander.
Variation Tip: You can add or omit spices according to your taste.
Nutritional Information per Serving: Calories: 467 | Fat: 19.9g | Sat Fat: 6.5g | Carbohydrates: 2.2g | Fiber: 1g | Sugar: 1g | Protein: 13g

Herbed Turkey Breast

⏰ **Prep Time:** 5 minutes 🍲 **Cook:** 50 minutes 🔖 **Serves:** 4

Ingredients:

3 tablespoons olive oil
1.8kg turkey breast
2 tablespoons garlic, minced
1 teaspoon thyme
1 teaspoon kosher salt
1 teaspoon rosemary
1 teaspoon basil

Preparation:

1. Switch the temperature of the Air fryer to 160°C. 2. In a bowl, merge the turkey breast with oil, herbs and garlic. 3. Layer the turkey breast in the Air fryer basket and then air fry for about 4. 50 minutes, flipping once in between. 5. Dish out and serve warm.
Serving Suggestions: Serve with roasted garlic and onions.
Variation Tip: You can use also use garlic powder instead of garlic.
Nutritional Information per Serving: Calories: 570 | Fat: 18.1g | Sat Fat: 3g | Carbohydrates: 20.9g | Fiber: 2.6g | Sugar: 16g | Protein: 77.7g

Simple Turkey Steaks

⏰ **Prep Time:** 5 minutes 🍲 **Cook:** 20 minutes 🔖 **Serves:** 4

Ingredients:

½ teaspoon salt
4 turkey breast steaks
½ teaspoon black pepper
1 teaspoon olive oil
1 teaspoon Italian seasoning

Preparation:

1. Switch the temperature of the Air fryer to 200°C. 2. In a bowl, rub turkey steaks with salt, pepper and Italian seasoning, and brush olive oil over it. 3. Layer the turkey steaks in the Air fryer basket and then air fry for about 20 minutes, flipping once in between. 4. Dish out and serve warm.
Serving Suggestions: Serve with pickled vegetables.
Variation Tip: You can also use Old Bay seasoning.
Nutritional Information per Serving: Calories: 122 | Fat: 1g | Sat Fat: 1g | Carbohydrates: 1g | Fiber: 1g | Sugar: 1g | Protein: 28g

Chicken and Veggie Skewers

⏱ **Prep Time:** 10 minutes   🍴 **Cook:** 10 minutes   🔖 **Serves:** 6

) Ingredients:

80ml sweet chili sauce
450g boneless skinless chicken breast, cut into bite sizes pieces
½ tablespoon Herbs de Provence
½ teaspoon red pepper flakes
1 teaspoon garlic granules

3 bell peppers, chopped
1 large onion, chopped
1 teaspoon smoked paprika
2 tablespoons vegetable oil
Salt and black pepper, to taste
1 courgette, chopped

) Preparation:

1. Switch the temperature of the Air fryer to 200°C. 2. Merge the chicken pieces with salt, black pepper, red pepper flakes. 3. Add courgette, bell peppers, onions, smoked paprika, herbs de Provence, sweet chili sauce, and vegetable oil, and thoroughly mix. 4. Marinate well for about half an hour, then thread chicken and vegetables on the skewers. 5. Layer the chicken skewers in the Air fryer basket and then air fry for about 10 minutes, flipping once in between. 6. Dish out and serve warm.

Serving Suggestions: You can serve with carrots and peas.
Variation Tip: You can use herbs of your choice.
Nutritional Information per Serving: Calories: 191 | Fat: 7g | Sat Fat: 4g | Carbohydrates: 14g | Fiber: 2g | Sugar: 1.5g | Protein: 18g

Air Fryer Curry Chicken Drumsticks

⏱ **Prep Time:** 35 minutes   🍴 **Cook:** 20 minutes   🔖 **Serves:** 4

) Ingredients:

¾ teaspoon salt, divided
450g chicken drumsticks
2 tablespoons olive oil
½ teaspoon onion salt

Minced fresh cilantro, optional
2 teaspoons curry powder
½ teaspoon garlic powder

) Preparation:

1. Switch the temperature of the Air fryer to 190°C. 2. Dissolve ½ teaspoon salt and some water to cover chicken legs. 3. Eliminate the legs from water and pat them dry. 4. In a bowl, merge the chicken legs with oil, onion salt, curry powder, garlic powder, and remaining ¼ teaspoon salt. 5. Layer the chicken legs in the Air fryer basket and then air fry for about 20 minutes, flipping once in between. 6. Dish out and serve garnished with cilantro.

Serving Suggestions: Serve with grilled potatoes and salad.
Variation Tip: You can add chili to increase spiciness.
Nutritional Information per Serving: Calories: 256 | Fat: 13.6g | Sat Fat: 2.7g | Carbohydrates: 0.9g | Fiber: 0.4g | Sugar: 0.1g | Protein: 31.4g

Crispy Turkey Escalope

⏱ **Prep Time:** 10 minutes   🍴 **Cook:** 25 minutes   🔖 **Serves:** 4

) Ingredients:

2 turkey escalopes
3 tablespoons flour

2 eggs
30g breadcrumbs

) Preparation:

1. Switch the temperature of the Air fryer to 200°C. 2. In a small bowl, place breadcrumbs. 3. In another bowl, whisk eggs and in a third bowl, spread flour. 4. Dip the turkey in the egg mixture after dredging them in the flour mixture. 5. Coat with the breadcrumbs and layer the turkey into the Air fryer basket. 6. Cook for 25 minutes, flipping once in between. 7. Dish out and serve warm.

Serving Suggestions: Serve with spaghetti.
Variation Tip: You can also use chicken instead of turkey.
Nutritional Information per Serving: Calories: 137 | Fat: 3.7g | Sat Fat: 1.2g | Carbohydrates: 10g | Fiber: 0.7g | Sugar: 0.7g | Protein: 15.8g

Cheese Turkey Meatballs

⏱ **Prep Time: 10 minutes** 🍲 **Cook: 12 minutes** ❖ **Serves: 6**

Ingredients:

160g onion, finely chopped
1 large egg
450g ground turkey
1 teaspoon garlic granules
30g panko breadcrumbs
1½ tablespoons mayonnaise, full-fat
Salt and black pepper, to taste
1 tablespoon Italian seasoning
50g Parmesan cheese, freshly grated
Fresh parsley, to serve

Preparation:

1. Switch the temperature of the Air fryer to 175°C. 2. In a bowl, merge ground turkey with onions, egg, garlic granules, Italian seasoning, mayonnaise, breadcrumbs, parmesan cheese, salt, and black pepper. 3. Thoroughly mix and form balls with this mixture. 4. Layer the meatballs in the Air fryer basket and then air fry for about 12 minutes, flipping once in between. 5. Dish out and serve warm.
Serving Suggestions: Serve with courgette noodles
Variation Tip: You can use pork rinds instead of breadcrumbs.
Nutritional Information per Serving: Calories: 243 | Fat: 13.3g | Sat Fat: 3.3g | Carbohydrates: 8.6g | Fiber: 1.2g | Sugar: 1.5g | Protein: 25.7g

Spiced Chicken with Bird's Eye Chilies

⏱ **Prep Time: 40 minutes** 🍲 **Cook: 25 minutes** ❖ **Serves: 2**

Ingredients:

1 teaspoon ginger, grated
340g chicken thighs, chopped
1 teaspoon garlic, grated
¼ teaspoon white pepper
4 tablespoons cornstarch
2 stalks bird's eye chilies
¼ teaspoon salt
½ teaspoon sugar
2 stalks curry leaves
Oil spray
Seasoning Powder:
½ teaspoon white pepper
½ teaspoon salt
¼ teaspoon five spice powder

Preparation:

1. Switch the temperature of the Air fryer to 180°C. 2. In a bowl, merge chicken thighs with ginger, garlic, salt, white pepper, and sugar. Marinate for 30 minutes. 3. Put curry leaves and bird's eye chilies in the Air fryer and then air fry for about 5 minutes. 4. Add cornstarch to the marinated chicken thighs until well-coated. 5. Layer the chicken in the Air fryer basket and then air fry for about 20 minutes, flipping once in between. 6. In a bowl, merge all the seasoning powder and add chicken and curry leaves. 7. Toss well and serve warm.
Serving Suggestions: Serve with potatoes and carrots.
Variation Tip: You can also make chicken breasts with this recipe.
Nutritional Information per Serving: Calories: 395 | Fat: 13g | Sat Fat: 3.6g | Carbohydrates: 16.3g | Fiber: 0.06g | Sugar: 0.1g | Protein: 49.5g

Crispy Breaded Chicken Breasts

⏱ Prep Time: 10 minutes   🍲 Cook: 15 minutes   ❧ Serves: 1

Ingredients:

1 egg
1 large chicken breast
2 tablespoons flour
¼ teaspoon garlic powder
¼ teaspoon black pepper
120g breadcrumbs
½ teaspoon salt
1 teaspoon olive oil

Preparation:

1. Switch the temperature of the Air fryer to 180°C. 2. In a small bowl, merge flour with garlic powder, salt, and black pepper. 3. In another bowl, whisk eggs and in a third bowl, spread breadcrumbs. 4. Dip the chicken in the egg mixture after dredging them in the flour mixture. 5. Coat with the breadcrumbs and layer the chicken into the Air fryer basket. 6. Spray with oil and cook for 15 minutes, flipping once in between. 7. Dish out and serve warm.

Serving Suggestions: Serve with cream cheese.
Variation Tip: You can use either fine white breadcrumbs or panko breadcrumbs.
Nutritional Information per Serving: Calories: 585 | Fat: 12.9g | Sat Fat: 2.1g | Carbohydrates: 75.3g | Fiber: 2.3g | Sugar: 0.6g | Protein: 39.5g

Air Fryer Chicken Meatballs

⏱ Prep Time: 10 minutes   🍲 Cook: 10 minutes   ❧ Serves: 6

Ingredients:

1 egg
450g ground chicken
60g breadcrumbs panko
1 tablespoon olive oil
1 teaspoon onion powder
½ teaspoon salt
1 tablespoon dried parsley
3 tablespoons parmesan cheese, grated
1 teaspoon garlic powder
1 teaspoon paprika
½ teaspoon black pepper

Preparation:

1. Switch the temperature of the Air fryer to 200°C. 2. In a bowl, merge ground chicken, egg, bread crumbs, parmesan cheese, garlic powder, paprika, onion powder, olive oil, parsley, salt, and black pepper. 3. Thoroughly mix and form balls with this mixture. 4. Layer the meatballs in the Air fryer basket and then air fry for about 10 minutes, flipping once in between. 5. Dish out and serve warm.

Serving Suggestions: Serve with orange wedges and pomegranate arils.
Variation Tip: You can also make chicken breast with this recipe.
Nutritional Information per Serving: Calories: 207 | Fat: 9.2g | Sat Fat: 2.3g | Carbohydrates: 6.1g | Fiber: 0.9g | Sugar: 0.5g | Protein: 24.2g

Paprika Chicken Thighs

🕐 **Prep Time: 10 minutes**   🍴 **Cook: 20 minutes**   ❧ **Serves: 6**

Ingredients:

1 tablespoon paprika
900g chicken thighs
⅛ teaspoon oregano
½ teaspoon brown sugar
¼ teaspoon garlic granules
Salt, to taste
½ teaspoon parsley
½ teaspoon cayenne
¼ teaspoon onion powder
1 tablespoon sunflower oil

Preparation:

1. Switch the temperature of the Air fryer to 180°C. 2. In a bowl, merge the chicken pieces with all the remaining ingredients and marinate for an hour. 3. Layer the chicken thighs in the Air fryer basket and then air fry for about 20 minutes, flipping once in between. 4. Dish out and serve warm.

Serving Suggestions: Serve with stir fried veggies.

Variation Tip: You can make this recipe with turkey thighs too.

Nutritional Information per Serving: Calories: 192 | Fat: 15g | Sat Fat: 4g | Carbohydrates: 1g | Fiber: 1g | Sugar: 1g | Protein: 12g

Air Fryer Spiced Chicken with Vegetables

🕐 **Prep Time: 10 minutes**   🍴 **Cook: 15 minutes**   ❧ **Serves: 4**

Ingredients:

1 small head broccoli, chopped
450g chicken thighs, boneless, chopped
1 small red bell pepper, chopped
1 small red onion
1 tablespoon parsley
Salt, to taste
½ teaspoon garlic granules
1 small yellow bell pepper, chopped
1 tablespoon paprika
1 teaspoon black pepper
1 tablespoon olive oil

Preparation:

1. Switch the temperature of the Air fryer to 175°C. 2. Dust the chicken with half the pepper, salt, olive oil, paprika, parsley, and garlic. Mix well. 3. Merge the vegetables with remaining black pepper, parsley, paprika, garlic, salt, and olive oil and thoroughly mix. 4. Layer the chicken and vegetables in the Air fryer basket and then air fry for about 15 minutes. 5. Dish out and serve warm.

Serving Suggestions: Serve over rice.

Variation Tip: You can use vegetables of your choice.

Nutritional Information per Serving: Calories: 349 | Fat: 20g | Sat Fat: 6g | Carbohydrates: 16g | Fiber: 5g | Sugar: 5g | Protein: 28g

Spiced Whole Duck

⏰ **Prep Time: 15 minutes** 🍲 **Cook: 1 hour 40 minutes** 🍃 **Serves: 4**

> **Ingredients:**

1½ teaspoons kosher salt
1.8kg whole duck
1 tablespoon dried parsley
2 teaspoons onion powder
3 teaspoons Cajun seasoning
2 teaspoons ginger powder
4 teaspoons dried basil
3 teaspoons paprika
3 teaspoons garlic powder
1 tablespoon olive oil

> **Preparation:**

1. Switch the temperature of the Air fryer to 160°C. 2. In a bowl, merge all the seasonings and apply to the duck inside out. 3. Position the duck on the Air fryer basket. 4. Cook for about 1 hour 40 minutes, flipping once in between. 5. Dish out and serve warm.

Serving Suggestions: Serve with coleslaw.

Variation Tip: You can also use any other variety of apples.

Nutritional Information per Serving: Calories: 437 | Fat: 36g | Sat Fat: 12g | Carbohydrates: 5g | Fiber: 2g | Sugar: 1.1g | Protein: 23g

Honey Mustard Glazed Chicken Wings

⏰ **Prep Time: 5 minutes** 🍲 **Cook: 20 minutes** 🍃 **Serves: 6**

> **Ingredients:**

60ml Dijon mustard
12 chicken wings
3 tablespoons honey
½ teaspoon garlic powder
½ teaspoon kosher salt
2 tablespoons butter, unsalted
½ teaspoon cayenne pepper

> **Preparation:**

1. Switch the temperature of the Air fryer to 200°C. 2. Layer the wings in the Air fryer basket and then air fry for about 20 minutes, flipping once in between. 3. Meanwhile, in a large bowl, merge Dijon mustard, honey, butter, cayenne pepper, garlic powder, and salt and cook for 10 minutes in a pan on low heat. 4. Add wings to the sauce and mix thoroughly. 5. Serve hot.

Serving Suggestions: Serve it with potato fries.

Variation Tip: You can also add some red chili flakes for more spiciness.

Nutritional Information per Serving: Calories: 624 | Fat: 40.3g | Sat Fat: 12.5g | Carbohydrates: 9.5g | Fiber: 0.4g | Sugar: 8.8g | Protein: 50.6g

Chapter 6 Beef, Pork, and Lamb Recipes

Air Fryer Beef Hamburgers

⏰ **Prep Time: 15 minutes**   🍲 **Cook: 8 minutes**   🥩 **Serves: 4**

Ingredients:

½ teaspoon salt
455g lean beef mince
½ teaspoon black pepper
¼ teaspoon garlic powder
½ teaspoon onion powder
60g barbecue sauce
For Serving
4 hamburger buns

Preparation:

1. Switch the temperature of the Air fryer to 185°C. 2. Merge the beef mince with salt, pepper, onion powder, and garlic powder. 3. Shape into patties and brush them with the barbecue sauce. 4. Layer the patties in the Air fryer basket and air fry for about 12 minutes, flipping once in between. 5. Dish out and serve warm inside buns.
Serving Suggestions: Serve with ketchup or salsa.
Variation Tip: You can also use your favorite rolls for serving.
Nutritional Information per Serving: Calories: 365 | Fat: 19g | Sat Fat: 7g | Carbohydrates: 22g | Fiber: 1g | Sugar: 3g | Protein: 25g

Herbed Roast Beef

⏰ **Prep Time: 5 minutes**   🍲 **Cook: 45 minutes**   🥩 **Serves: 4**

Ingredients:

Seasoning:
2 teaspoons coarse salt
½ teaspoon dried thyme
½ teaspoon dried rosemary
1 teaspoon black pepper
½ teaspoon garlic granules
½ teaspoon brown sugar
For the Roast Beef:
3 tablespoons olive oil
1.1kg roasting beef joint

Preparation:

1. Switch the temperature of the Air fryer to 200°C. 2. Merge all the seasoning ingredients and scrub the beef with this seasoning mixture and oil. 3. Layer the beef in the Air fryer basket and air fry for about 45 minutes, flipping once in between. 4. Dish out and serve warm.
Serving Suggestions: Serve with pickled onions.
Variation Tip: You can also use mustard powder instead of brown sugar.
Nutritional Information per Serving: Calories: 125 | Fat: 11g | Sat Fat: 2g | Carbohydrates: 2g | Fiber: 1g | Sugar: 1g | Protein: 4g

Herbed Steak Bites

⏰ **Prep Time: 5 minutes**   🍲 **Cook: 12 minutes**   🍖 **Serves: 4**

Ingredients:

2 tablespoons olive oil
900g steak, cut into small pieces
1 teaspoon garlic powder

Salt and cracked pepper, to taste
½ teaspoon Herbs de Provence

Preparation:

1. Switch the temperature of the Air fryer to 200°C. 2. Dust the steak bites with herb de Provence, garlic powder, salt, black pepper, olive oil and thoroughly mix. 3. Layer the steak bites in the Air fryer basket and then air fry for about 12 minutes, flipping once in between. 4. Dish out and serve tossed with garlic butter.

Serving Suggestions: Serve with pickled onions.
Variation Tip: You can replace herb de Provence with any other herbs of choice.
Nutritional Information per Serving: Calories: 536 | Fat: 39g | Sat Fat: 15g | Carbohydrates: 1g | Fiber: 1g | Sugar: 1g | Protein: 46g

Tasty Shepherd's Pie

⏰ **Prep Time: 15 minutes**   🍲 **Cook: 1 hour 15 minutes**   🍖 **Serves: 4**

Ingredients:

1 large onion, chopped
1 tablespoon sunflower oil
3 medium carrots, chopped
2 tablespoons tomato purée
480ml beef stock

185g butter
455g pack lamb mince
1 large splash Worcestershire sauce
900g potatoes, cut into chunks and boiled
3 tablespoons milk

Preparation:

1. Switch the temperature of the Air fryer to 200°C. 2. In a saucepan, cook onions and carrots in sunflower oil for 5 minutes. 3. Add lamb mince, tomato purée and Worcestershire sauce. Cook for about 8 minutes. 4. Stir in the beef stock and cook for 40 minutes 5. Mash the potatoes with butter and milk. 6. In the Air fryer baking pan, add the mince and top with the potato mash. 7. Place in the Air fryer and air fry for about 20 minutes. 8. Dish out and serve warm.

Serving Suggestions: Serve with mashed potatoes.
Variation Tip: You can also use butter instead of oil.
Nutritional Information per Serving: Calories: 663 | Fat: 39g | Sat Fat: 20g | Carbohydrates: 49g | Fiber: 5g | Sugar: 10g | Protein: 33g

Tasty Rib-Eye Steak

⏰ **Prep Time: 15minutes**   🍲 **Cook: 10 minutes**   🍖 **Serves: 2**

Ingredients:

1 teaspoon paprika
2 ribeye steak
½ teaspoon oregano
Salt, to taste
½ teaspoon black pepper

Preparation:

1. Switch the temperature of the Air fryer to 200°C. 2. In a bowl, merge steaks with paprika, oregano, salt, and black pepper. Mix well. 3. Layer the steaks in the Air fryer basket and then air fry for about 10 minutes, flipping once in between. 4. Dish out in a platter and serve warm.

Serving Suggestions: Serve with garlic herb butter.
Variation Tip: You can use any cut of steak, sirloin, or tri-tip.
Nutritional Information per Serving: Calories: 581 | Fat: 43g | Sat Fat: 21g | Carbohydrates: 2g | Fiber: 1g | Sugar: 1g | Protein: 46g

Pork Belly with Golden Syrup Sauce

🕐 Prep Time: 15 minutes 🍲 Cook: 20 minutes 🥗 Serves: 8

Ingredients:

1 tablespoon brown sugar
900g pork belly, boneless
3 teaspoons smoked paprika
1 teaspoon onion powder
Golden Syrup Sauce:
2 tablespoons golden syrup
56g butter
2 tablespoons barbecue sauce

1 teaspoon olive oil
2 teaspoons plain flour
½ teaspoon garlic powder

2 teaspoons Sriracha
1 tablespoon bourbon

Preparation:

1. Switch the temperature of the Air fryer to 200°C. 2. In a bowl, merge sugar, paprika, flour, oil, onion, and garlic powder. 3. Layer the pork belly in the Air fryer basket and then air fry for about 20 minutes, flipping once in between. 4. Meanwhile, merge butter, golden syrup, barbecue sauce, bourbon, and Sriracha to make the golden syrup sauce. 5. Transfer the sauce into a pan and simmer for about 7 minutes. 6. Dish out the pork belly bites and serve drizzled with golden syrup sauce.

Serving Suggestions: Serve with pickled vegetables.
Variation Tip: You can use garlic instead of garlic powder.
Nutritional Information per Serving: Calories: 611 | Fat: 36.5g | Sat Fat: 16.8g | Carbohydrates: 8g | Fiber: 0.4g | Sugar: 3.7g | Protein: 52.7g

Herbed Lamb Ribs

🕐 Prep Time: 10 minutes 🍲 Cook: 10 minutes 🥗 Serves: 8

Ingredients:

8 lamb ribs
For Seasoning:
60ml olive oil
1 teaspoon thyme
2 garlic cloves, minced

1 teaspoon rosemary
1 teaspoon oregano
Salt and black pepper, to taste

Preparation:

1. Switch the temperature of the Air fryer to 150°C. 2. In a bowl, merge all the seasoning ingredients and coat over lamb ribs. 3. Layer the lamb ribs in the Air fryer basket and then air fry for about 10 minutes, flipping once in between. 4. Dish out in a platter and serve warm.

Serving Suggestions: Serve with vegetable sauté or salads.
Variation Tip: You can also use seasoning of your choice.
Nutritional Information per Serving: Calories: 425 | Fat: 27.5g | Sat Fat: 8.5g | Carbohydrates: 0.6g | Fiber: 0.2g | Sugar: 0g | Protein: 41.7g

Easy Air Fryer Porterhouse Steaks

🕐 Prep Time: 2 minutes 🍲 Cook: 10 minutes 🥗 Serves: 2

Ingredients:

2 (225g) porterhouse steaks
1 teaspoon olive oil
Salt and black pepper, to taste

Preparation:

1. Switch the temperature of the Air fryer to 160°C. 2. In a bowl, rub the steaks with olive oil, salt and black pepper. 3. Layer the steaks in the Air fryer basket and then air fry for about 10 minutes, flipping once in between. 4. Dish out in a platter and serve warm.

Serving Suggestions: Serve with roasted garlic and chili.
Variation Tip: You can use coconut aminos instead of soy sauce.
Nutritional Information per Serving: Calories: 477 | Fat: 24g | Sat Fat: 9.2g | Carbohydrates: 0g | Fiber: 0g | Sugar: 0g | Protein: 61.2g

Herbed Lamb Chops with Garlic Sauce

⏰ **Prep Time:** 15 minutes   🍲 **Cook:** 22 minutes   🍃 **Serves:** 4

Ingredients:

3 tablespoons olive oil
1 garlic bulb
1 tablespoon fresh oregano, finely chopped
8 lamb chops
Sea salt and black pepper, to taste

Preparation:

1. Switch the temperature of the Air fryer to 200°C. 2. Position the garlic bulb in the Air fryer basket and coat with olive oil. 3. Cook for about 12 minutes and keep aside. 4. In a bowl, merge herbs, sea salt, pepper and olive oil. 5. Coat half of the herb oil mixture over the lamb chops. 6. Mix the remaining herb oil mixture with garlic. 7. Layer the lamb chops in the Air fryer basket and then air fry for about 10 minutes, flipping once in between. 8. Dish out in a platter and serve with garlic sauce.

Serving Suggestions: Serve with couscous and braised courgette.
Variation Tip: You can use pork chops instead of lamb chops.
Nutritional Information per Serving: Calories: 706 | Fat: 34.6g | Sat Fat: 10.1g | Carbohydrates: 1.5g | Fiber: 0.5g | Sugar: 0.1g | Protein: 91.9g

Mustard Pork Chops with Potatoes

⏰ **Prep Time:** 15 minutes   🍲 **Cook:** 25 minutes   🍃 **Serves:** 4

Ingredients:

1½ teaspoons olive oil
12 baby potatoes, halved
2 teaspoons honey
½ teaspoon ground paprika
2 teaspoons fresh thyme leaves
1 teaspoon Dijon mustard
4 pork cutlets

Preparation:

1. Switch the temperature of the Air fryer to 185°C. 2. In a bowl, merge pork chops with oil, honey, mustard and paprika. Mix well. 3. Layer the potatoes in the Air fryer basket and then air fry for about 10 minutes, flipping once in between. 4. Now, add pork chops to the Air fryer and cook for 12 minutes, tossing once in between. 5. Dish out and serve sprinkled with thyme.

Serving Suggestions: Serve with potatoes and steamed broccolini.
Variation Tip: You can also use your favorite rolls for serving.
Nutritional Information per Serving: Calories: 331 | Fat: 7.1g | Sat Fat: 1.3g | Carbohydrates: 56.2g | Fiber: 4.1g | Sugar: 3.4g | Protein: 9.4g

Easy Air Fryer Lamb Steaks

⏰ **Prep Time:** 5 minutes   🍲 **Cook:** 12 minutes   🍃 **Serves:** 2

Ingredients:

2 lamb steaks, 1-inch thick
1 teaspoon salt and black pepper
½ tablespoon light olive oil

Preparation:

1. Switch the temperature of the Air fryer to 200°C. 2. In a bowl, dust the lamb steaks with salt and black pepper, and scrub with oil. 3. Layer the lamb steaks in the Air fryer basket and then air fry for about 12 minutes, flipping once in between. 4. Dish out in a platter and serve warm.

Serving Suggestions: Serve with piccalilli or your favorite pickle.
Variation Tip: You can use any seasoning of your choice.
Nutritional Information per Serving: Calories: 469 | Fat: 31g | Sat Fat: 11g | Carbohydrates: 0g | Fiber: 0g | Sugar: 0g | Protein: 43g

Simple Herb Roast Beef

⏱ **Prep Time: 5 minutes** 🍲 **Cook: 30 minutes** 🍴 **Serves: 4**

Ingredients:

1 teaspoon black pepper
2 teaspoons coarse salt
½ teaspoon dried thyme
½ teaspoon dried rosemary
½ teaspoon garlic granules
½ teaspoon brown sugar
For the Roast Beef:
3 tablespoons olive oil
70g roasting beef joint

Preparation:

1. Switch the temperature of the Air fryer to 200°C. 2. In a bowl, merge the beef with all the seasoning ingredients. 3. Layer the beef in the Air fryer basket and then air fry for about 15 minutes, flipping once in between. 4. Switch the temperature of the Air fryer to 175°C. 5. Cook for about 15 minutes and dish out to serve.
Serving Suggestions: Serve with steamed broccoli.
Variation Tip: You can also use mustard powder instead of brown sugar.
Nutritional Information per Serving: Calories: 125 | Fat: 11g | Sat Fat: 2g | Carbohydrates: 2g | Fiber: 1g | Sugar: 1g | Protein: 4g

Air Fryer Steaks with Sweet Potatoes & Mushrooms

⏱ **Prep Time: 10 minutes** 🍲 **Cook: 35 minutes** 🍴 **Serves: 6**

Ingredients:

60ml crème Fraîche
450g sweet potatoes, peeled, cut into wedges
1 tablespoon milk
2 teaspoons fresh tarragon, chopped
1 small green shallot, finely chopped
4 large flat mushrooms
1 tablespoon horseradish sauce
2 (225g) porterhouse steaks
56g garlic butter, chopped
1 tablespoon olive oil

Preparation:

1. Switch the temperature of the Air fryer to 180°C. 2. In a bowl, merge crème Fraîche with milk, shallot, horseradish sauce, and garlic butter. 3. Position the sweet potatoes in the Air fryer basket and then air fry for about 20 minutes, flipping once in between. 4. Dish out and keep aside. 5. Layer the steaks in the Air fryer basket and then air fry for about 10 minutes, flipping once in between. 6. Dish out and keep aside with sweet potatoes. 7. Layer the mushrooms in the Air fryer basket and sprinkle with butter, oil, and tarragon. 8. Cook for about 5 minutes, flipping once in between. 9. Dish out with steak, sweet potatoes and mushrooms and serve drizzled with crème fraîche mixture.
Serving Suggestions: Serve with watercress.
Variation Tip: You can also use red potatoes instead of sweet potatoes.
Nutritional Information per Serving: Calories: 312 | Fat: 16.3g | Sat Fat: 6.6g | Carbohydrates: 17.9g | Fiber: 2.7g | Sugar: 5.3g | Protein: 22.8g

Sweet & Sour Flank Steak

⏱ **Prep Time: 5 minutes** 🍴 **Cook: 10 minutes** ☰ **Serves: 4**

Ingredients:

680g Flank Steak
60ml balsamic dressing
1 teaspoon ground garlic
½ teaspoon red pepper flakes
60ml soy sauce, low sodium
50g brown sugar
2 tablespoons Worcestershire sauce
Salt and pepper, to taste

Preparation:

1. Switch the temperature of the Air fryer to 200°C. 2. In a bowl, merge steaks with all other ingredients. Mix well. 3. Layer the steaks in the Air fryer basket and then air fry for about 10 minutes, flipping once in between. 4. Dish out in a platter and serve warm.
Serving Suggestions: Serve with roasted asparagus.
Variation Tip: You can also serve with your favorite sauce.
Nutritional Information per Serving: Calories: 409 | Fat: 16.8g | Sat Fat: 5.9g | Carbohydrates: 12.6g | Fiber: 0.2g | Sugar: 10.6g | Protein: 48.4g

Homemade Beef Jerky

⏱ **Prep Time: 5 minutes** 🍴 **Cook: 20 minutes** ☰ **Serves: 4**

Ingredients:

450g beef sirloin steak, thinly sliced into strips
Marinade:
120ml Worcestershire sauce   120ml soy sauce
1 tablespoon honey   1 teaspoon onion powder
½ teaspoon chili flakes

Preparation:

1. Switch the temperature of the Air fryer to 180°C. 2. In a bowl, merge the beef slices with all the marinade ingredients. Mix well. 3. Layer the beef strips in the Air fryer basket and then air fry for about 20 minutes, flipping once in between. 4. Dish out in a platter and serve warm.
Serving Suggestions: Serve with roasted veggies.
Variation Tip: You can also use maple syrup instead of honey.
Nutritional Information per Serving: Calories: 276 | Fat: 7.1g | Sat Fat: 2.7g | Carbohydrates: 13.3g | Fiber: 0.3g | Sugar: 11.1g | Protein: 36.5g

Air Fryer Mustard Pork Tenderloin

⏱ **Prep Time: 30 minutes** 🍴 **Cook: 30 minutes** ☰ **Serves: 3**

Ingredients:

1 pork tenderloin
1 tablespoon Dijon Mustard
2 tablespoons brown sugar
1 teaspoon paprika
1 teaspoon onion powder
¼ teaspoon black pepper
¼ teaspoon salt
½ teaspoon garlic powder
1 teaspoon Frank's Red Hot sauce

Preparation:

1. Switch the temperature of the Air fryer to 195°C. 2. In a bowl, merge the pork tenderloin with all the remaining ingredients. Marinate well. 3. Layer the pork chops in the Air fryer basket and then air fry for about 30 minutes, flipping once in between. 4. Dish out in a platter and serve warm.
Serving Suggestions: Serve with red radishes.
Variation Tip: You can also use red chili flakes for added spiciness.
Nutritional Information per Serving: Calories: 175 | Fat: 4.1g | Sat Fat: 1.4g | Carbohydrates: 3.8g | Fiber: 0.3g | Sugar: 3.2g | Protein: 29.3g

Simple Pork Steaks

⏰ **Prep Time: 5 minutes** 🍲 **Cook: 10 minutes** 🍃 **Serves: 4**

) Ingredients:

1 tablespoon vegetable oil
4 pork steaks, about 1 inch thick
1½ tablespoons pork seasoning
Salt and black pepper, to taste

) Preparation:

1. Switch the temperature of the Air fryer to 200°C. 2. In a bowl, dust both sides of the pork steaks with pork rub, salt and black pepper, and scrub with oil. 3. Layer the pork steaks in the Air fryer basket and then air fry for about 10 minutes, flipping once in between. 4. Dish out in a platter and serve warm.
Serving Suggestions: Serve over cooked rice.
Variation Tip: You can substitute vegetable oil with any other flavorless cooking oil.
Nutritional Information per Serving: Calories: 200 | Fat: 11.4g | Sat Fat: 3.7g | Carbohydrates: 0g | Fiber: 0g | Sugar: 0g | Protein: 22g

Rack of lamb with Mint Pesto

⏰ **Prep Time: 15 minutes** 🍲 **Cook: 15 minutes** 🍃 **Serves: 4**

) Ingredients:

1 bunch fresh mint
2 racks of lamb
2 garlic cloves
1 tablespoon honey
60ml olive oil, extra virgin
Salt and black pepper, to taste

) Preparation:

1. Switch the temperature of the Air fryer to 200°C. 2. In a blender, blitz mint, garlic, oil, and honey, salt and black pepper to form mint pesto. 3. Merge the rack of lamb with mint pesto. Marinate well. 4. Layer the rack of lamb in the Air fryer basket and then air fry for about 15 minutes, flipping once in between. 5. Dish out in a platter and serve warm.
Serving Suggestions: Serve with mashed potatoes and fresh vegetables.
Variation Tip: You can also use maple syrup instead of honey.
Nutritional Information per Serving: Calories: 440 | Fat: 24.8g | Sat Fat: 6.1g | Carbohydrates: 6.8g | Fiber: 1.6g | Sugar: 4.3g | Protein: 46.8g

Chapter 7 Dessert Recipes

Cheesecake

⏲ **Prep Time: 10 minutes   Cook time: 10 minutes   Serves: 2**

Ingredients:

100g cream cheese, softened
2 tablespoons erythritol
1 tablespoon all-natural, no-sugar-added peanut

butter
½ teaspoon vanilla extract
1 large egg, whisked

Preparation:

1. In a medium bowl, mix cream cheese and erythritol until smooth. Add peanut butter and vanilla, mixing until smooth. Add egg and stir just until combined. 2. Spoon the mixture into an ungreased 10 cm spring-form nonstick pan and place into air fryer basket. 3. Air-fry the mixture at 150°C for 10 minutes until the edges are firm, but centre will be mostly set with only a small amount of jiggle when done. 4. Let pan cool at room temperature 30 minutes, cover with plastic wrap, then place into refrigerator at least 2 hours. Serve chilled.

Serving Suggestions: Serve chilled with fresh berries, a drizzle of sugar-free chocolate sauce, or a dollop of whipped cream for an extra treat.

Variation Tip: Swap peanut butter with almond butter or hazelnut spread for a different flavor. Add a pinch of cinnamon or lemon zest to the batter for a zesty twist.

Nutritional Information per Serving: Calories: 223 | Fat: 20.71g | Sat Fat: 11.9g | Carbohydrates: 3.16g | Fiber: 0.4g | Sugar: 2.38g | Protein: 6.55g

Raspberry Chocolate Lava Cake

⏲ **Prep Time: 15 minutes   Cook time: 15 minutes   Serves: 4**

Ingredients:

50g semisweet chocolate chips
40g milk chocolate chips
55g butter
2 large eggs
1 large egg yolk
50g granulated sugar
3 tablespoons icing sugar
1 teaspoon vanilla

4 tablespoons plain flour
¼ teaspoon baking powder
Pinch sea salt
Unsalted butter, at room temperature
2 teaspoons cocoa powder
4 teaspoons raspberry jam
125g fresh raspberries
1 tablespoon freshly squeezed lemon juice

Preparation:

1. In a small microwave-safe bowl, melt the semisweet chocolate chips, milk chocolate chips, and butter in the microwave on medium power for 2 to 3 minutes. Remove and stir until combined and smooth, then set aside. 2. In a medium bowl, beat together the eggs and egg yolk. Gradually add the granulated and icing sugars, beating until the mixture is fluffy and lighter yellow in colour. Beat in the vanilla. 3. Add the flour, baking powder, and salt and mix until combined. Then fold in the chocolate and butter mixture. 4. Grease four 100g glass heatproof ramekins with the unsalted butter. Sprinkle ½ teaspoon cocoa power in each ramekin and shake to coat. Shake out the excess cocoa powder. 5. Fill the ramekins half full with the batter. Top each with a teaspoon of the raspberry jam. Cover the jam with the rest of the batter. 6. Place the ramekins in the air fryer basket. You may be able to bake all four at one time, or just two at a time, depending on the size of your machine. 7. Preheat the air fryer to 190°C. Put the basket in the air fryer. Bake the food for 9 to 12 minutes or until the edges of the cake are set. 8. While the cakes are baking, place the raspberries and lemon juice in a small saucepan. Bring to a simmer over medium-low heat. Simmer for 2 to 4 minutes or until a sauce forms. Remove from heat and set aside. 9. Remove the basket from the air fryer and let the ramekins cool on a wire rack for 5 minutes. Run a knife around the edge of each ramekin and invert each cake onto a serving plate. Top with the sauce and serve.

Serving Suggestions: Serve warm with a dollop of whipped cream or a scoop of vanilla ice cream.

Variation Tip: Substitute raspberry jam with strawberry or orange marmalade for a fruity twist. For a nutty flavor, sprinkle crushed hazelnuts or almonds on top before serving.

Nutritional Information per Serving: Calories: 368 | Fat: 19.63g | Sat Fat: 11.7g | Carbohydrates: 47g | Fiber: 3.7g | Sugar: 35.57g | Protein: 4.81g

Mini Cherry Tart

⏱ **Prep Time: 30 minutes**   🍲 **Cook: 40 minutes**   ❧ **Serves: 12**

Ingredients:

275g sheets of short crust pastry
For the Filling:
50g of softened butter
50g of golden caster sugar
1 egg
1 tablespoon plain flour
50g ground almonds
25g cherry jam
For the Icing:
60g icing sugar
Glazed cherries for topping

Preparation:

1. Switch the air fryer to 150°C. 2. Grease a muffin tin that fits in the air fryer 3. Spread the pastry and cut circles. Line these in the muffin molds. Push them down and fix them. 4. Chill it in the fridge for 10 minutes. Then bake it in the air fryer for 20 minutes until golden brown. Remove from the air fryer and let them cool. Remove from the mold and set it aside. 5. For the filling: Beat sugar with butter until light. Add up egg and flour. Fold almonds and jam in the mixture. 6. Fill the mixture in each shell. 7. Bake in the air fryer for another 20 minutes till the filling is firm and brown. 8. For the icing: Mix the icing sugar with a tablespoon of water and spread it on the tarts. 9. Put glazed cherries on top and serve.

Serving Suggestions: Serve with Tea
Variation Tip: You can also use walnuts instead of almonds.
Nutritional Information per Serving: Calories: 534 | Fat: 30g | Sat Fat: 12g | Carbohydrates: 57g | Fiber: 2g | Sugar: 32g | Protein: 6g

Fluffy Orange Soufflé

⏱ **Prep Time: 5 minutes**   🍲 **Cook: 10 minutes**   ❧ **Serves: 6**

Ingredients:

3 egg whites
5 tablespoons castor sugar
3 egg yolks
1 large orange (zest and juice)
2 tablespoons powdered sugar
Orange Curd Filling:
1 egg
1 orange (zest and juice)
50g granulated sugar
1 teaspoon cornstarch
2 tablespoons unsalted butter

Preparation:

1. Preheat your oven to 190°C. Grease 2 ramekins. 2. Mix egg, orange juice, and zest with cornstarch until light and fluffy. 3. Heat butter in a saucepan and add the egg mixture. Mix until the custard thickens. Set it aside and let it cool. 4. Beat egg whites with powdered sugar until fluffy. 5. Beat egg yolks separately with castor sugar until it turns pale. Add orange juice and zest. Fold the egg white and egg yolk mixture gently. 6. Mix the egg mixture with curd and fold gently with a spatula. 7. Add the mixture to the prepared ramekins and bake in the air fryer for 10 minutes. 8. Serve.

Serving Suggestions: Dust with powdered sugar while serving.
Variation Tip: You can add orange extract for a more pungent orangey taste.
Nutritional Information per Serving: Calories: 451 | Fat: 20.7g | Sat Fat: 10.4g | Carbohydrates: 56.5g | Fiber: 2.2g | Sugar: 52.1g | Protein: 13.2g

Bread and Raisin Pudding

⏰ Prep Time: 20 minutes   🍲 Cook: 20 minutes   🌿 Serves: 6

Ingredients:

240ml milk
1 egg
1 tablespoon brown sugar
½ teaspoon ground cinnamon
¼ teaspoon vanilla extract
2 tablespoons raisins, soaked in hot water for about 15 minutes
2 bread slices, cut into small cubes
1 tablespoon chocolate chips
1 tablespoon sugar

Preparation:

1. Mix milk, egg, brown sugar, cinnamon, and vanilla extract well in a bowl. 2. Stir in the raisins. 3. In a baking dish, spread the bread cubes and top evenly with the milk mixture. 4. Refrigerate for about 15-20 minutes. 5. Switch the air fryer to 190°C. 6. Remove from refrigerator and sprinkle with chocolate chips and sugar on top. 7. Arrange the baking dish into an air fryer basket. 8. Air fry for about 12 minutes. 9. Once done, serve warm.

Serving Suggestions: You can serve with custard.
Variation Tip: You can use any bread.
Nutritional Information per Serving: Calories: 143 | Fat: 4.4g | Sat Fat: 1.3g | Carbohydrates: 21.3g | Fiber: 1g | Sugar: 16.4g | Protein: 5.5g

Raspberry Cupcakes

⏰ Prep Time: 30 minutes   🍲 Cook: 20 minutes   🌿 Serves: 12

Ingredients:

75g butter, softened
190g plain flour
1 teaspoon vanilla extract
5 eggs, 4 separated
300g golden or white caster sugar
1 teaspoon baking powder
150ml milk
12 teaspoons raspberry jam
35g raspberries

Preparation:

1. Switch the air fryer to 150°C and preheat for 10 minutes. 2. Line a 6-hole cupcake pan with the cupcake liners and set aside. 3. Beat sugar and butter until fluffy. Add vanilla extract, an egg, and four egg yolks and beat well to combine. 4. Add flour, baking powder, and milk to the egg mixture. 5. Fill cupcake liners with cake mixture until it is half filled. Add 1 teaspoon of jam to each cupcake mixture. Fill the cupcake batter until it is filled ⅔rd. Smooth out the top. 6. Bake in the air fryer for 20 minutes. 7. Meanwhile, prepare meringue by beating egg whites with 1 cup of granulated sugar until stiff peaks form. 8. Pipe meringue on the cupcakes and color them with the blow torch. Garnish with raspberry and serve.

Serving Suggestions: Serve with tea
Variation Tip: If you don't have a blow torch, you can air fry the meringue for 10 minutes until it is firm.
Nutritional Information per Serving: Calories: 374 | Fat: 20g | Sat Fat: 12g | Carbohydrates: 47g | Fiber: 1g | Sugar: 36g | Protein: 6g

Apple Oatmeal Cookies

⏰ Prep Time: 10 minutes   🍲 Cook: 20 minutes   🍃 Serves: 6

Ingredients:

57g butter, plus a little for greasing
1 teaspoon cinnamon
40g raisins
90g porridge oats
60g pelt flour
2 tablespoons maple syrup
125g grated apple
30g unblanched hazelnuts, cut into chunky slices
1 egg

Preparation:

1. Switch the air fryer to 200°C. 2. Grease the air fryer tray with butter and set aside. 3. Microwave butter and syrup together until it is melted. 4. In a saucepan, add melted butter, syrup, and apples. Cook for one minute until it is softened. Add cinnamon and raisins as well. 5. Mix oats, flour, and hazelnuts in a bowl and transfer the cooked apple mixture to that. Beat an egg and combine everything well until the mixture comes together. 6. Scoop out the mixture into the tray and cook for 18 minutes until golden brown. 7. Cook the remaining batch in the same manner.

Serving Suggestions: Serve with cinnamon apple tea.
Variation Tip: You can add almonds as well.
Nutritional Information per Serving: Calories: 146 | Fat: 8g | Sat Fat: 3g | Carbohydrates: 15g | Fiber: 2g | Sugar: 8g | Protein: 2g

Pear, Blackberry, and Pistachio Crumble

⏰ Prep Time: 10 minutes   🍲 Cook: 35 minutes   🍃 Serves: 4

Ingredients:

4 large ripe pears, peeled and cubed
150g blackberry
200g golden granulated sugar
227g unsalted butter, cold, cut into small pieces
120g shelled pistachio, roughly chopped
125g plain flour
100g demerara sugar
Ice cream, to serve (optional)
Salt, to taste

Preparation:

1. Switch the air-fryer to 175°C and preheat for 10 minutes. 2. In a saucepan, cook sugar and pears until soft. Add blackberries and wait until the mixture boils. 3. Divide the fruit mixture into the ramekins and set aside. 4. Mix butter, flour, and salt in a bowl until the mixture is crumbly. Add sugar and pistachios and mix well. 5. Sprinkle the crumble mixture over the filled ramekins. Freeze it for one hour and then cook it in the air fryer for about 35 minutes or until it turns golden brown. 6. Serve warm, and enjoy.

Serving Suggestions: serve with vanilla ice cream
Variation Tip: You can also use hazelnuts instead of pistachios.
Nutritional Information per Serving: Calories: 768 | Fat: 33g | Sat Fat: 15g | Carbohydrates: 115g | Fiber: 0g | Sugar: 76g | Protein: 10g

Toffee Apple Bread with Cream Pudding

⏲ **Prep Time:** 10 minutes   🍴 **Cook:** 40 minutes   🍃 **Serves:** 4

Ingredients:

3 red dessert apples, cored and diced
Juice of ½ lemon, about 1 tablespoon
4 tablespoons caster sugar
1 can of caramel, 397g
6 brioche finger rolls, cut in chunks
3 eggs
375ml full-fat milk
240ml double cream
1 teaspoon vanilla extract

Preparation:

1. Switch the air fryer to 200°C. Preheat for 5 minutes. 2. Toss apples with lemon juice to prevent coloring. 3. Take a deep dish that fits in the air fryer and spread caramel in the base. 4. Layer the chunks of bread and diced apples on top of the caramel. Drizzle more caramel on top. 5. Whisk milk, cream, eggs, sugar, and vanilla with the hand mixer. 6. Pour this mixture on the bread and bake it in the air fryer. 7. It should be firm and brown after 40 minutes. 8. Serve warm.

Serving Suggestions: Serve with vanilla ice cream
Variation Tip: You can add raisins as well.
Nutritional Information per Serving: Calories: 831 | Fat: 37g | Sat Fat: 21g |
Carbohydrates: 105g | Fiber: 2g | Sugar: 70g | Protein: 18g

Traditional Cranachan

⏲ **Prep Time:** 15 minutes   🍴 **Cook:** 20 minutes   🍃 **Serves:** 2

Ingredients:

250g fresh British raspberries
2 tablespoons medium oatmeal
1 tablespoon caster sugar
360ml double cream
2 tablespoons honey
2-3 tablespoons whisky, to taste

Preparation:

1. Switch the air-fryer to 200°C and preheat for 10 minutes. 2. Toast the oatmeal by air frying it for 20 minutes. It should smell nutty and turn a bit darker in color. 3. For the syrup, blend half of the raspberries and strain through the sieve. Add the caster sugar and mix well. 4. Whisk double cream with whisky and honey. Stir the oatmeal in the cream. 5. Assemble cranachan by layering raspberry sauce, fresh raspberries, and cream mixture. 6. Serve.

Serving Suggestions: serve it chilled.
Variation Tip: You can add roasted walnuts or pecans as well
Nutritional Information per Serving: Calories: 529 | Fat: 48g | Sat Fat: 27g |
Carbohydrates: 18g | Fiber: 2g | Sugar: 13g | Protein: 3g

Orange and Lemon Tangy Pie

⏰ **Prep Time:** 30 minutes   🍲 **Cook:** 20 minutes   🍃 **Serves:** 6

Ingredients:

310g ready to cook short-crust pastry
For the Filling:
1 large egg
4 large egg yolks
397g light condensed milk
2 teaspoons lemon juice
80ml orange juice
1 teaspoon lemon zest
2 teaspoons of orange zest
For the Topping:
160ml extra-thick double cream
250g Greek yoghurt
4 tablespoons icing sugar
More lemon and orange zest to decorate

Preparation:

1. Switch the air fryer to 175°C and preheat for 10 minutes. 2. Roll the pastry and line four tart tins with the pastry. 3. Bake the base in the air fryer for 15 minutes until it turns golden. 4. Whisk egg yolks and egg in a bowl until it turns pale. Add condensed milk along with zests and juices of orange and lemon. 5. Pour in the cooked pastry shells and bake them for 20 minutes in an oven. 6. Once the filling is formed, leave it in the fridge for one hour. You can also leave it in the refrigerator overnight. 7. For the topping, whisk all the topping ingredients until thick. Then, pipe it on the chilled pies. 8. Serve cold.

Serving Suggestions: Garnish with lemon zest and spring flowers.
Variation Tip: You can use low-fat Greek yoghurt as well.
Nutritional Information per Serving: Calories: 647 | Fat: 27g | Sat Fat: 15g | Carbohydrates: 87g | Fiber: 1g | Sugar: 63g | Protein: 12g

Banana Cake

⏰ **Prep Time:** 5 minutes   🍲 **Cook:** 40 minutes   🍃 **Serves:** 8

Ingredients:

For the Topping:
300g light muscovado sugar
½ teaspoon vanilla bean paste
115 unsalted butter, plus extra for greasing
4 large bananas
For the Cake Batter:
310g plain flour
3 large eggs
160ml soured cream
1 teaspoon cinnamon
½ teaspoon ground ginger
400g golden caster sugar
150g softened unsalted butter
2½ teaspoons baking powder

Preparation:

1. Switch the air fryer to 150°C and preheat for 10 minutes. 2. Grease a baking pan with butter. 3. Heat butter, vanilla, and sugar on medium heat until sugar is melted. Pour this caramel sauce into the base of the pan. 4. Cut the bananas lengthwise and arrange them in the base of the cake pan. 5. For the cake batter, beat all the ingredients with the electric mixer until well combined. 6. Pour the batter on top of the bananas and smoothen them out with the spatula. 7. Bake in the air fryer for 40 minutes until the cake is cooked from the center. 8. Remove from the air fryer. Let it cool for some time. 9. Invert the cake into the serving dish and serve.

Serving Suggestions: Serve with egg custard
Variation Tip: You can use dark brown sugar for the base.
Nutritional Information per Serving: Calories: 427 | Fat: 18g | Sat Fat: 11g | Carbohydrates: 62g | Fiber: 2g | Sugar: 45g | Protein: 5g

Banana Bread with Vanilla Ricotta & Raspberries Compote

⏱ **Prep Time: 30 minutes**   🍲 **Cook: 30 minutes**   🍃 **Serves: 8**

Ingredients:

For the Banana Bread:
2-3 very ripe bananas (mashed)
150g butter, softened
150g light muscovado sugar
2 large eggs
¼ teaspoon lemon zest
1 teaspoon vanilla extract
180ml buttermilk
310g self-raising flour
1 teaspoon ground cinnamon
½ teaspoon bicarbonate of soda
For the Vanilla Ricotta:
255g tub of ricotta
3 teaspoons vanilla bean paste
Juice of 2 oranges
¼ teaspoon of orange zest
For the Raspberry Compote:
Juice of 2 oranges
200g granulated sugar
450g raspberries

Preparation:

1. Switch the air fryer to 150°C. Grease a loaf pan. 2. Beat sugar and butter until fluffy. Beat eggs, mashed bananas, lemon zest, buttermilk, and vanilla extract. 3. Add flour, baking soda, and ground cinnamon to the butter mixture. 4. Bake the cake mixture in the air fryer for 30 minutes. 5. When it's cooked, let it cool. Slice into 8 slices. 6. Beat all the ingredients of ricotta frosting for 3-4 minutes. Once done, chill in the fridge. 7. For the raspberry compote, cook raspberries along with orange juice and sugar. Once the syrup thickens, keep it aside and chill. 8. Grill banana bread slices in the air fryer at 85°C. 9. Serve warm slices with ricotta cheese and raspberry compote.

Serving Suggestions: Garnish with fresh raspberries and serve with coffee
Variation Tip: You can use full-fat milk instead of buttermilk.
Nutritional Information per Serving: Calories: 483 | Fat: 20g | Sat Fat: 12g | Carbohydrates: 63g | Fiber: 4g | Sugar: 42g | Protein: 9g

Maple Pears with Roasted Pecan Nuts

⏱ **Prep Time: 5 minutes**   🍲 **Cook: 25 minutes**   🍃 **Serves: 4**

Ingredients:

4 ripe pears
2 tablespoons maple syrup, plus extra to serve
60g pecan nuts, broken roughly

Preparation:

1. Switch the air fryer to 40°C and preheat for 5 minutes. 2. Core pears and cut them in half. Place them into a dish along with maple syrup. Cover with foil and bake in the air fryer for 20 minutes. 3. Pears should be soft by then. Once cooked, set it aside. 4. Roast pecans in the air fryer for 4 minutes. Remove and coarsely chop them. 5. Sprinkle on pears and serve.

Serving Suggestions: serve with Greek yoghurt
Variation Tip: You can use hazelnuts as well. Sprinkle cinnamon on the pears for variation in taste.
Nutritional Information per Serving: Calories: 209 | Fat: 9g | Sat Fat: 1g | Carbohydrates: 32g | Fiber: 4g | Sugar: 9g | Protein: 2g

Hazelnut Cookies

⏰ Prep Time: 25 minutes 🍲 Cook: 18 minutes ❖ Serves: 12

Ingredients:

140g hazelnut
65g plain flour
200g caster sugar
2 eggs
½ teaspoon vanilla extract

Preparation:

1. Switch the air-fryer to 150°C. 2. Mix all the ingredients with an electric mixer until a dough is formed. 3. Line an air fryer tray with parchment paper. 4. Scoop out cookies on the tray and bake for 18 minutes. 5. Once cooked, remove and bake the rest of the dough in batches.

Serving Suggestions: Serve with coffee.

Variation Tip: You can use self-raising flour as well

Nutritional Information per Serving: Calories: 51 | Fat: 2g | Sat Fat: 0g | Carbohydrates: 8g | Fiber: 0g | Sugar: 7g | Protein: 1g

Easy Gingerbread Bundt Cake

⏰ Prep Time: 15 minutes 🍲 Cook: 30 minutes ❖ Serves: 6

Ingredients:

310g all-purpose flour
1 teaspoon salt
1 teaspoon baking soda
1 teaspoon ginger
340g molasses
1 large egg
50g granulated sugar
240ml buttermilk
3 tablespoons butter melted and unsalted

Preparation:

1. Switch the air-fryer to 160°C and preheat for 10 minutes. 2. Mix the flour, salt, ground ginger, and baking soda in a large bowl. 3. Then mix in the egg, buttermilk, molasses, sugar, and butter. 4. Mix well and spray the baking pan with olive oil spray. 5. Let the mixture bake in the air fryer for 30 minutes.

Serving Suggestions: Dust icing sugar while serving.

Variation Tip: You can use mixed spices for variation in taste.

Nutritional Information per Serving: Calories: 320 | Fat: 2g | Sat Fat: 1g | Carbohydrates: 69g | Fiber: 1g | Sugar: 40g | Protein: 6g

Conclusion

Our journey with the air fryer has been both enlightening and transformative. This amazing appliance is not just about giving a healthier twist to guilty pleasures; it's about reshaping our cooking experience. The recipes serve as mere stepping stones, inviting you to push boundaries, tweak ingredients, and perhaps even pioneer some air-fried masterpieces. Don't be confined by written instructions; the true essence of cooking lies in experimentation and personal touches.

As we wrap up, envision the air fryer as a kitchen gadget and a canvas for future culinary adventures. Its potential is yet to be fully realized, and as the culinary world continues to evolve, so will the wonders of air frying. Remember, every dish you cook adds to this ongoing experience. So, as you enjoy countless healthier and tasty meals, take a moment to celebrate the innovation that the air fryer brings to your kitchen. Continue exploring!

Appendix Recipes Index

Printed in Great Britain
by Amazon

56601012R00044